Tween Coloring Books For Girls

Stress Relief Vol 1

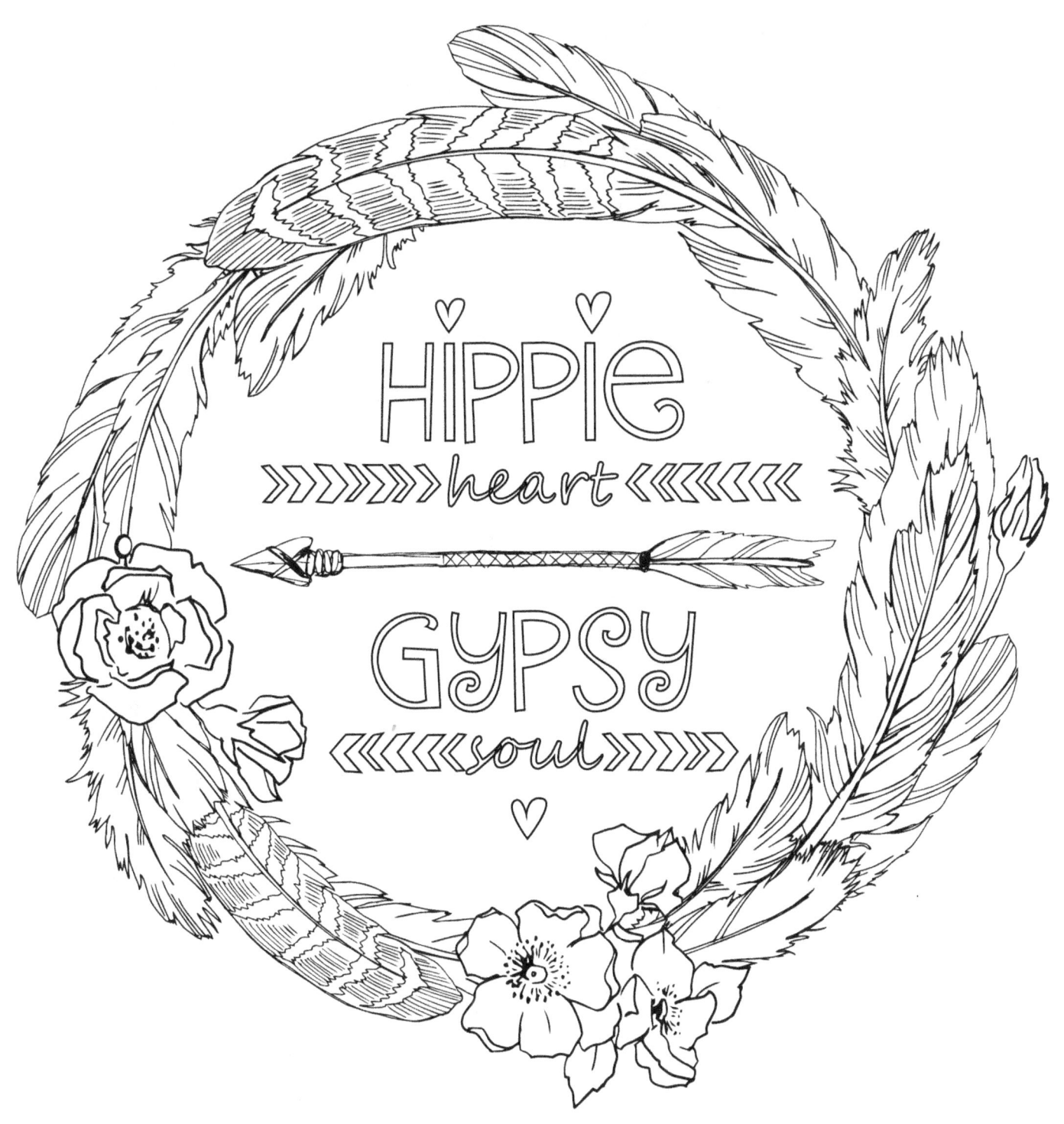

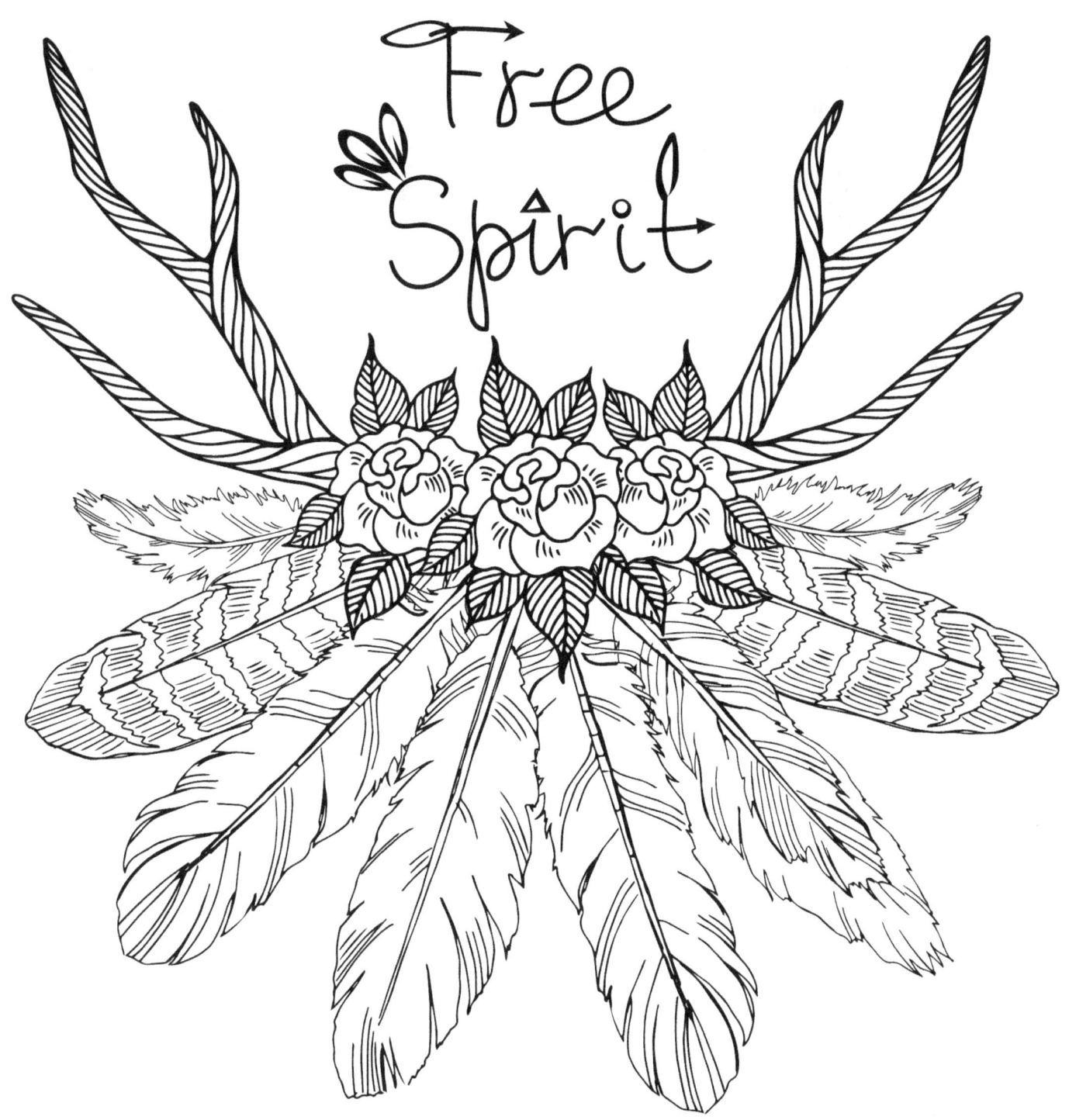

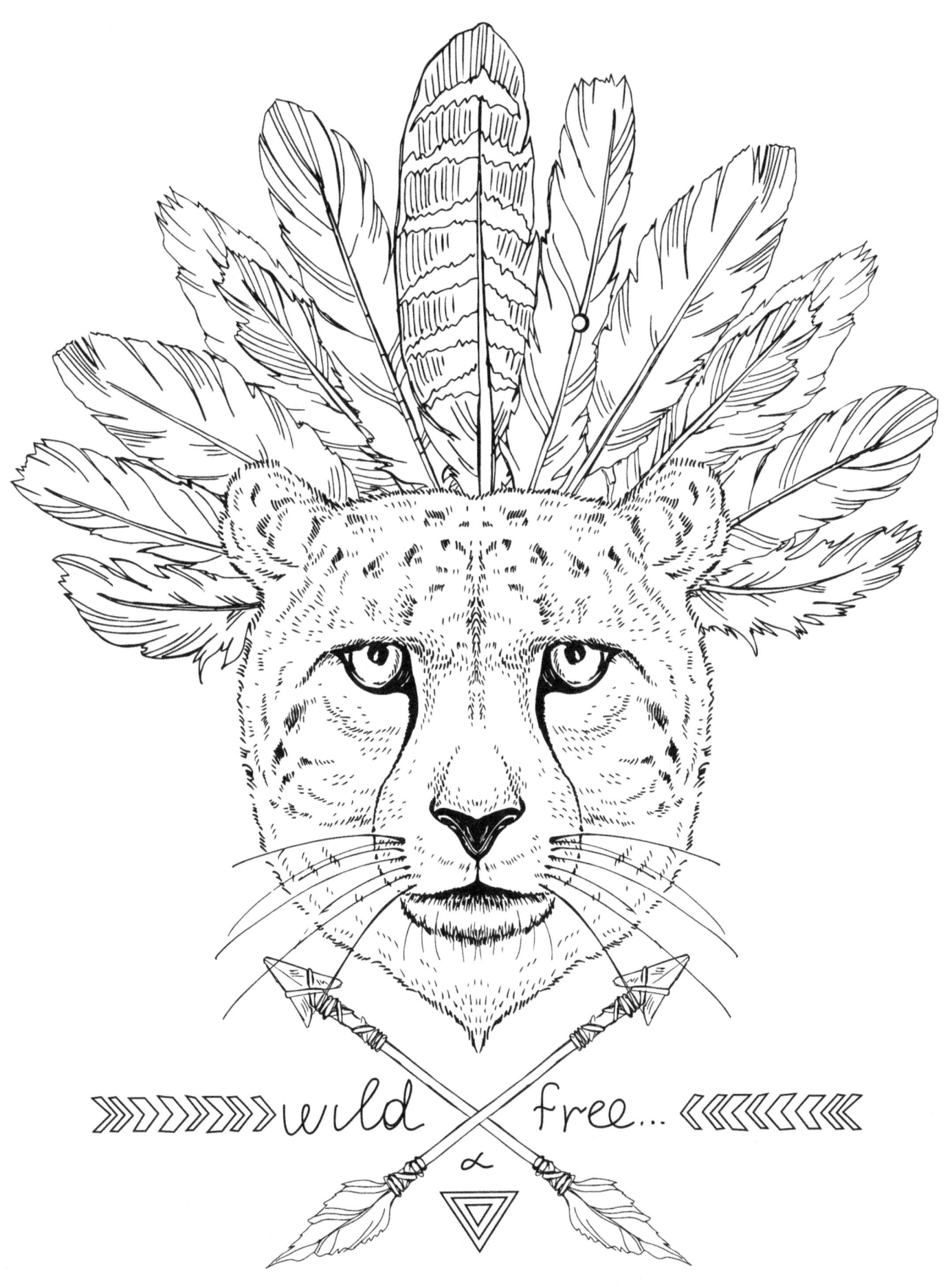

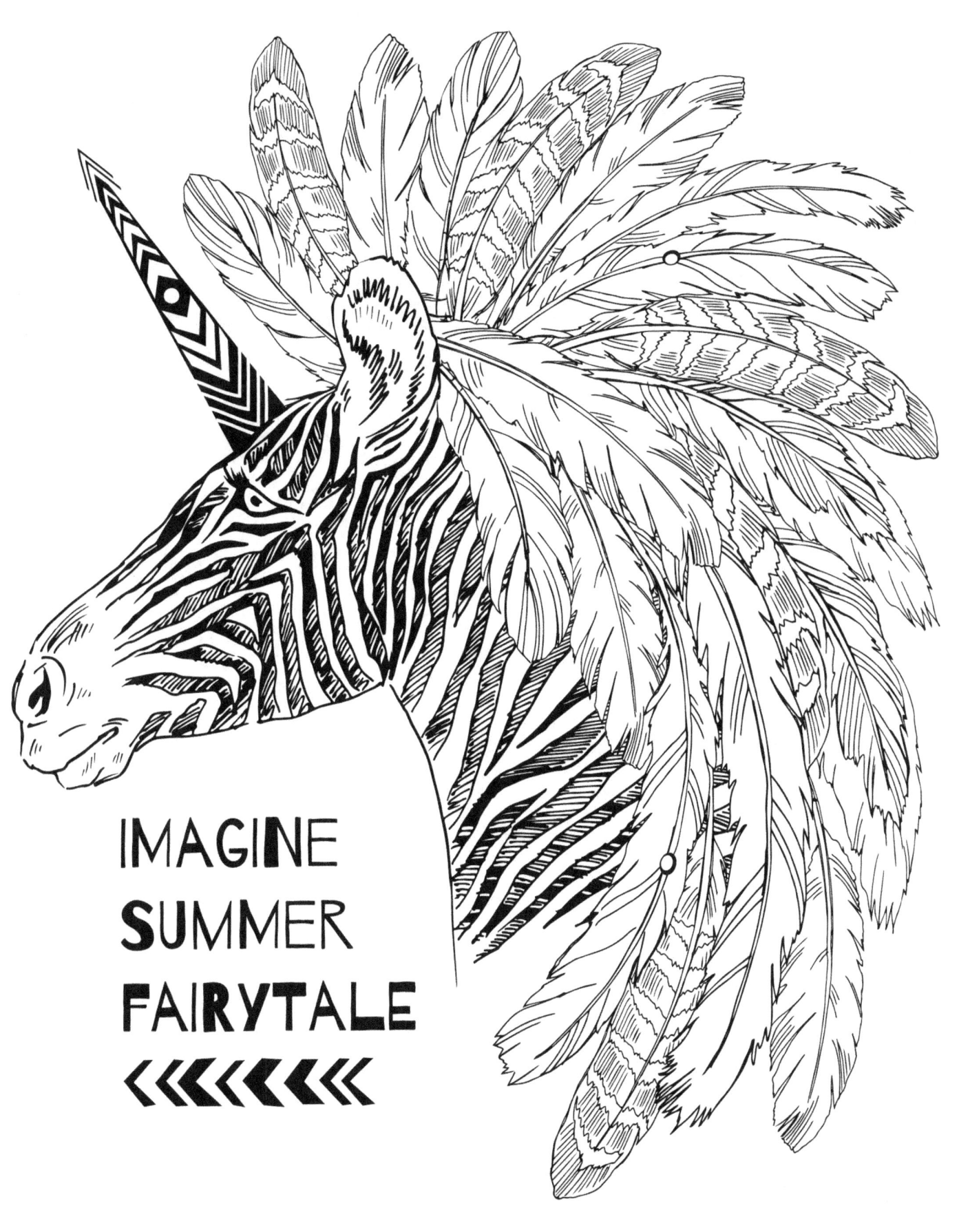

IMAGINE
SUMMER
FAIRYTALE
<<<<<<<

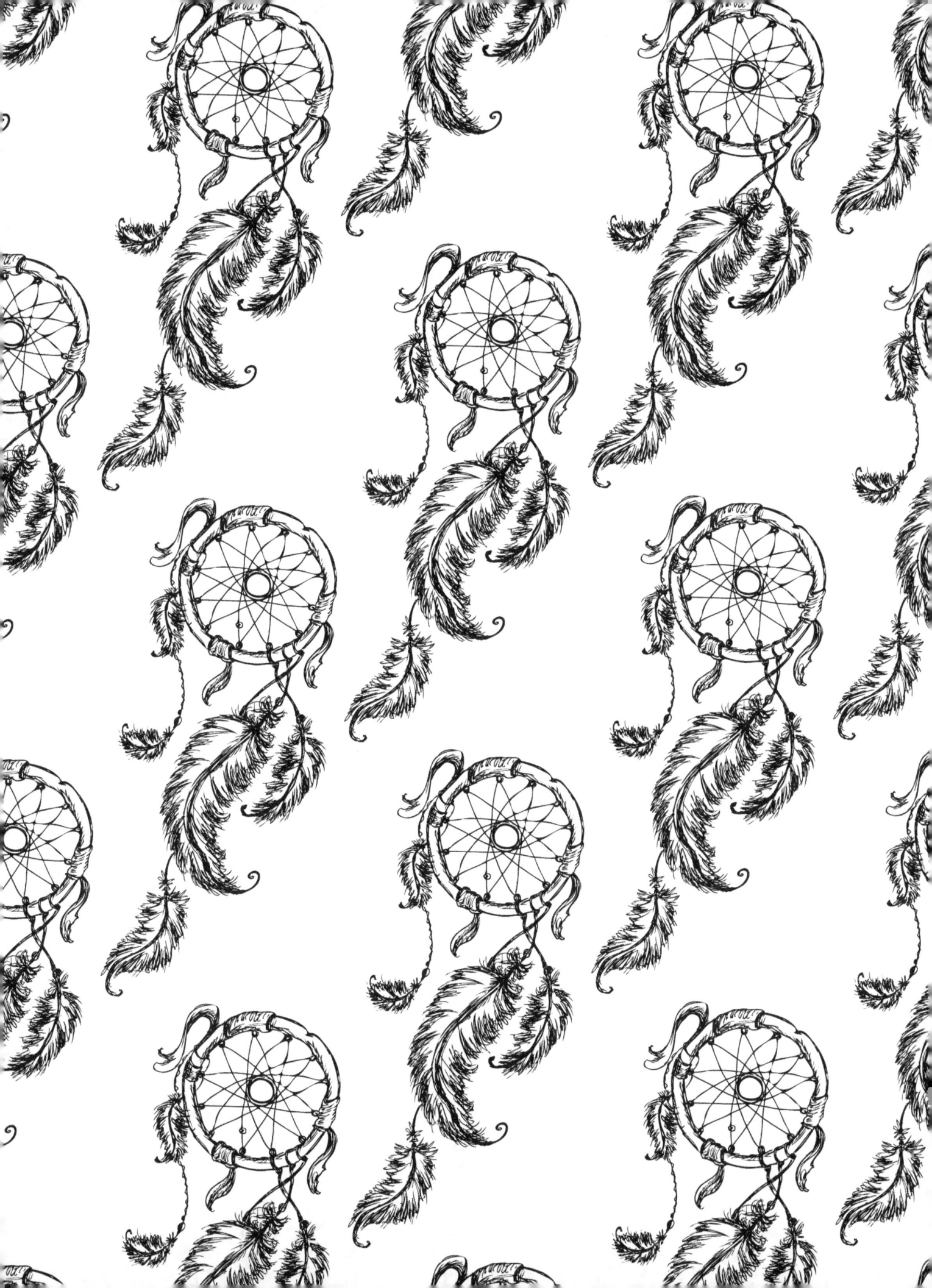

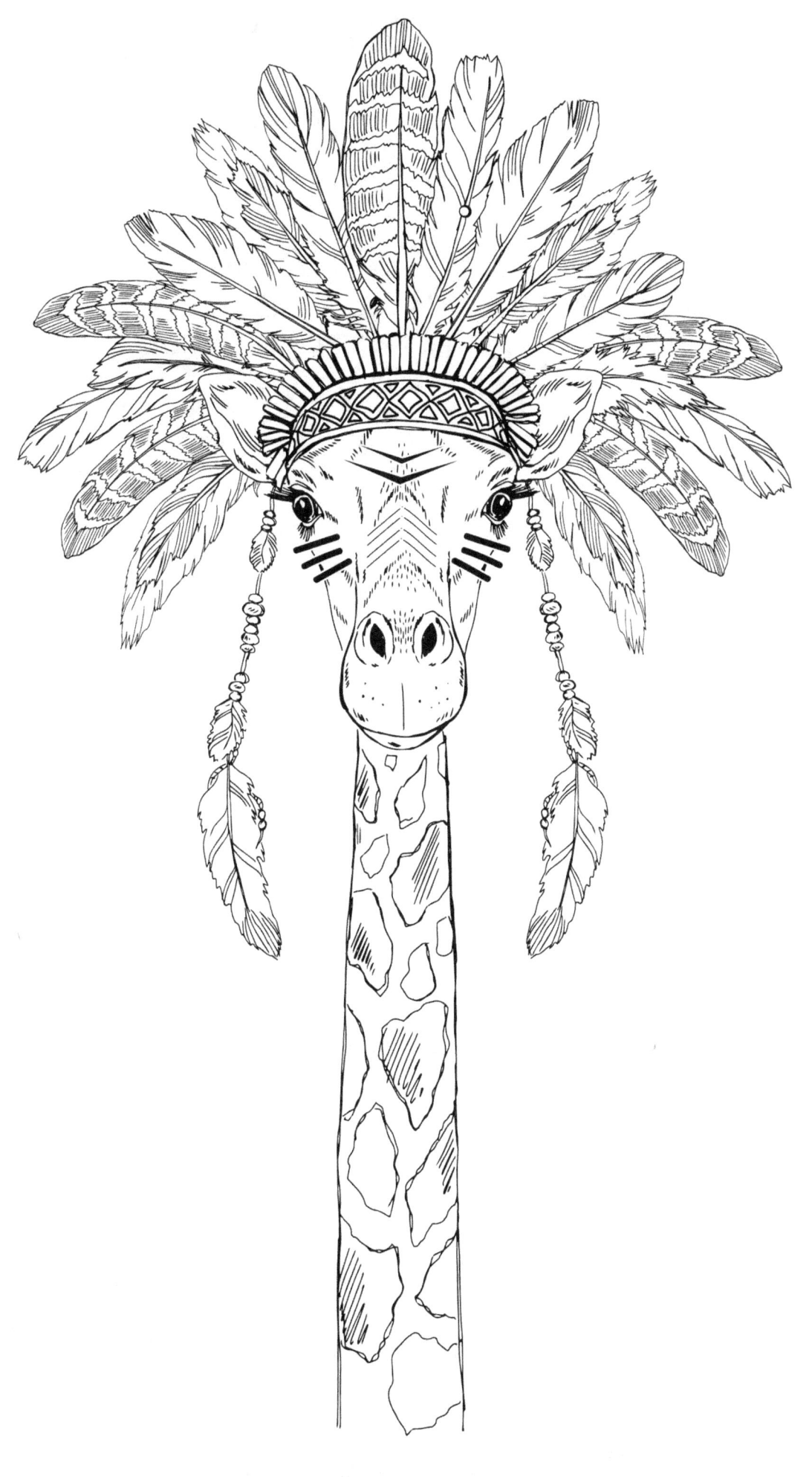

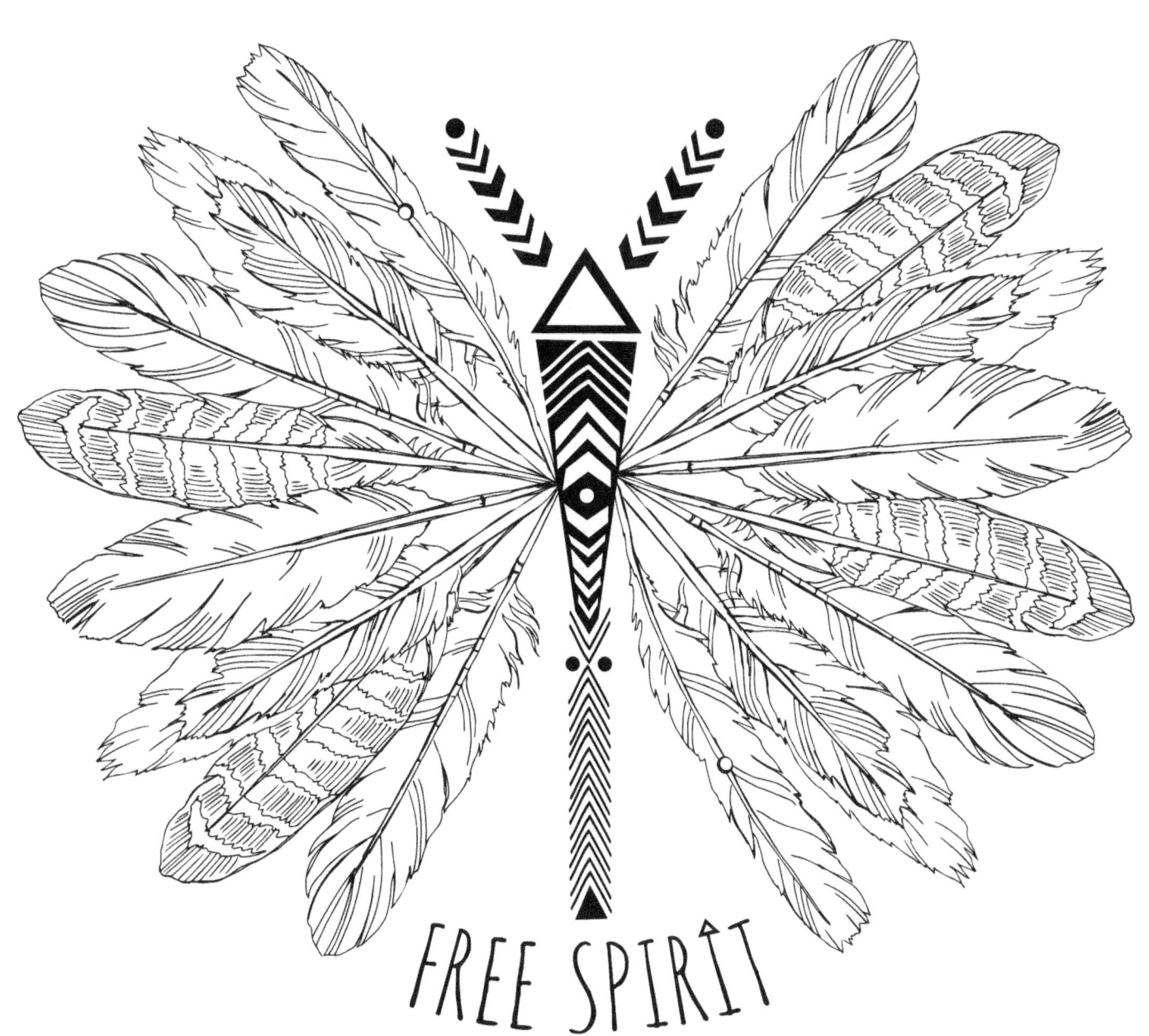

FREE SPIRIT

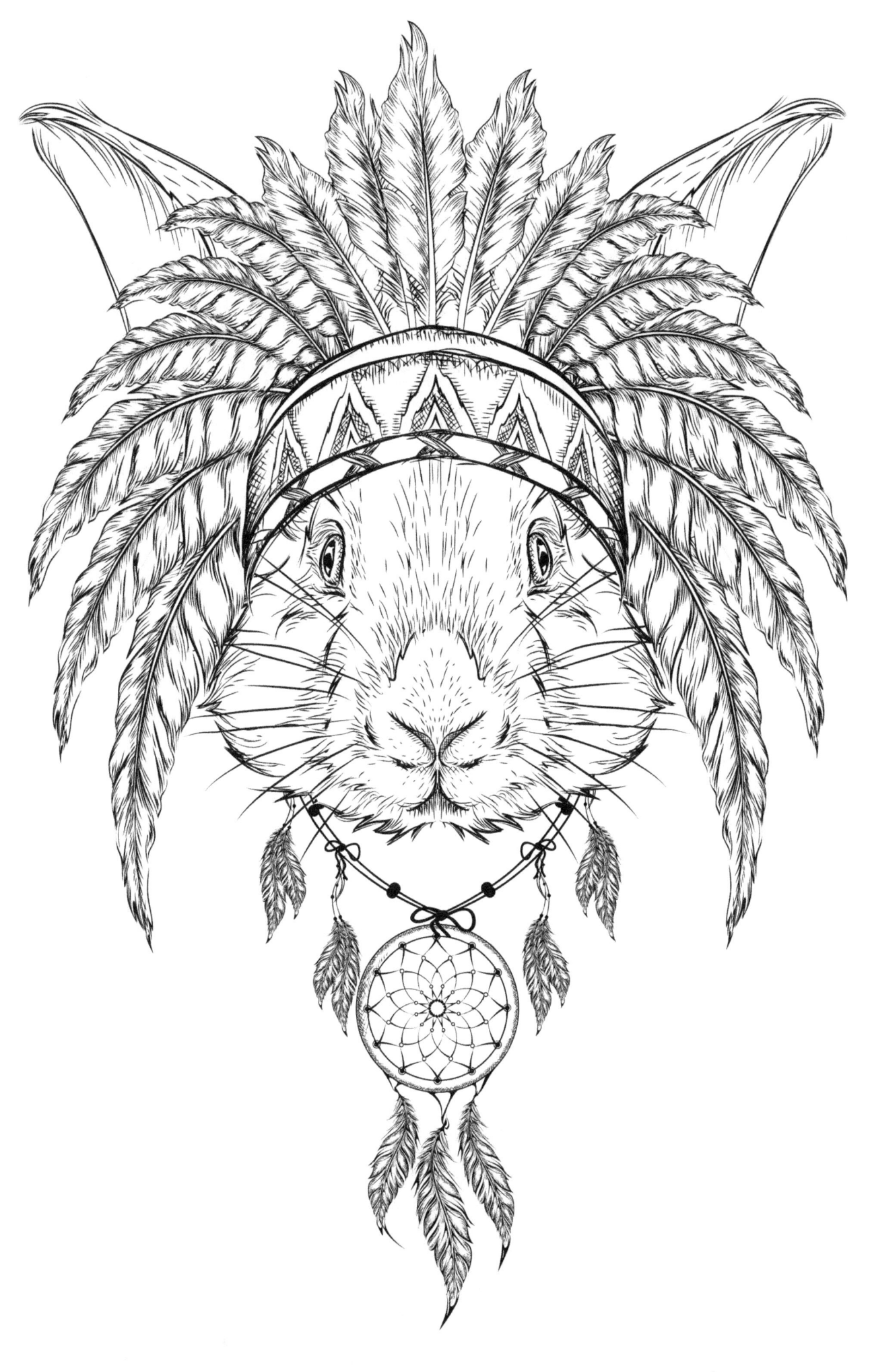

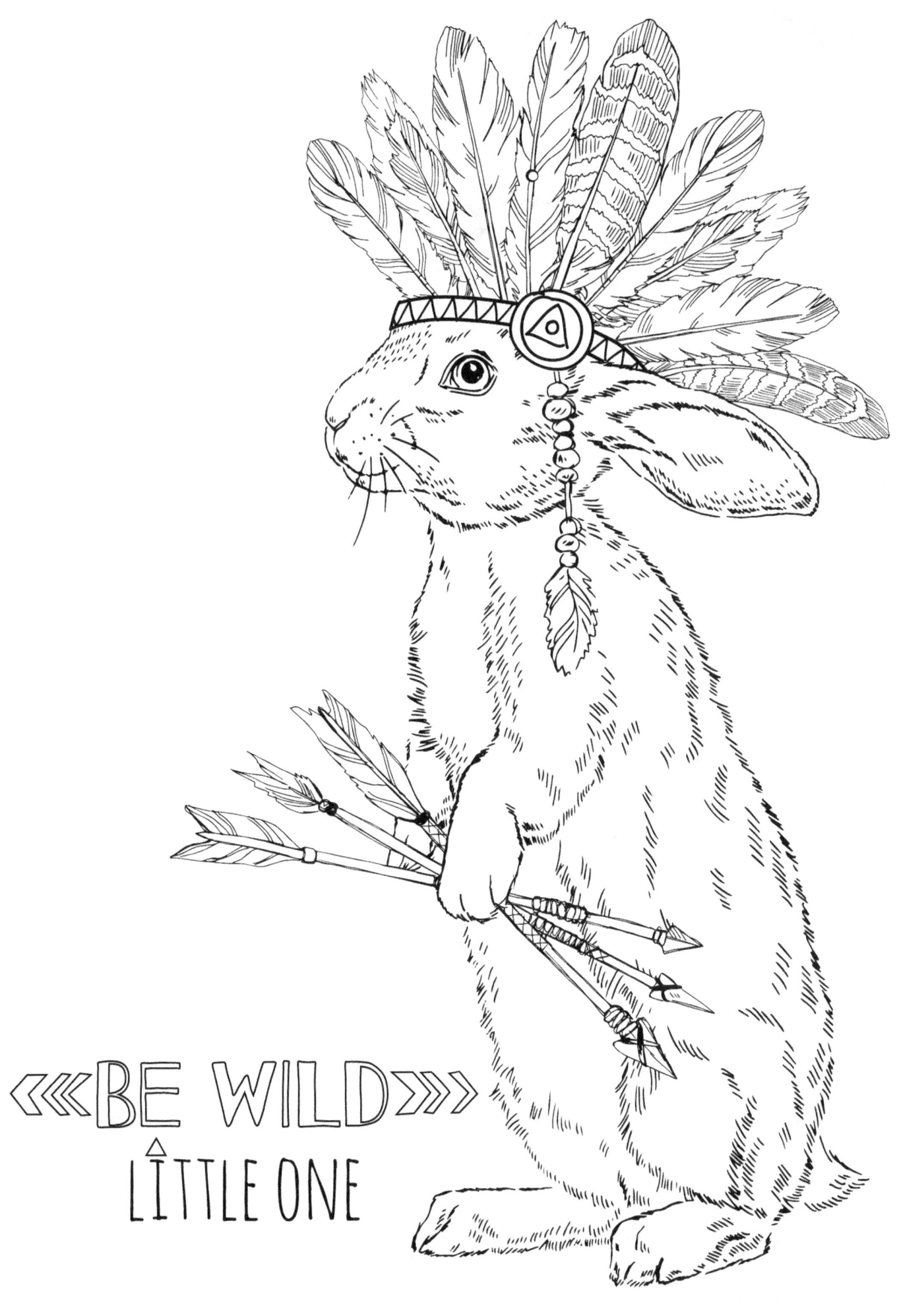

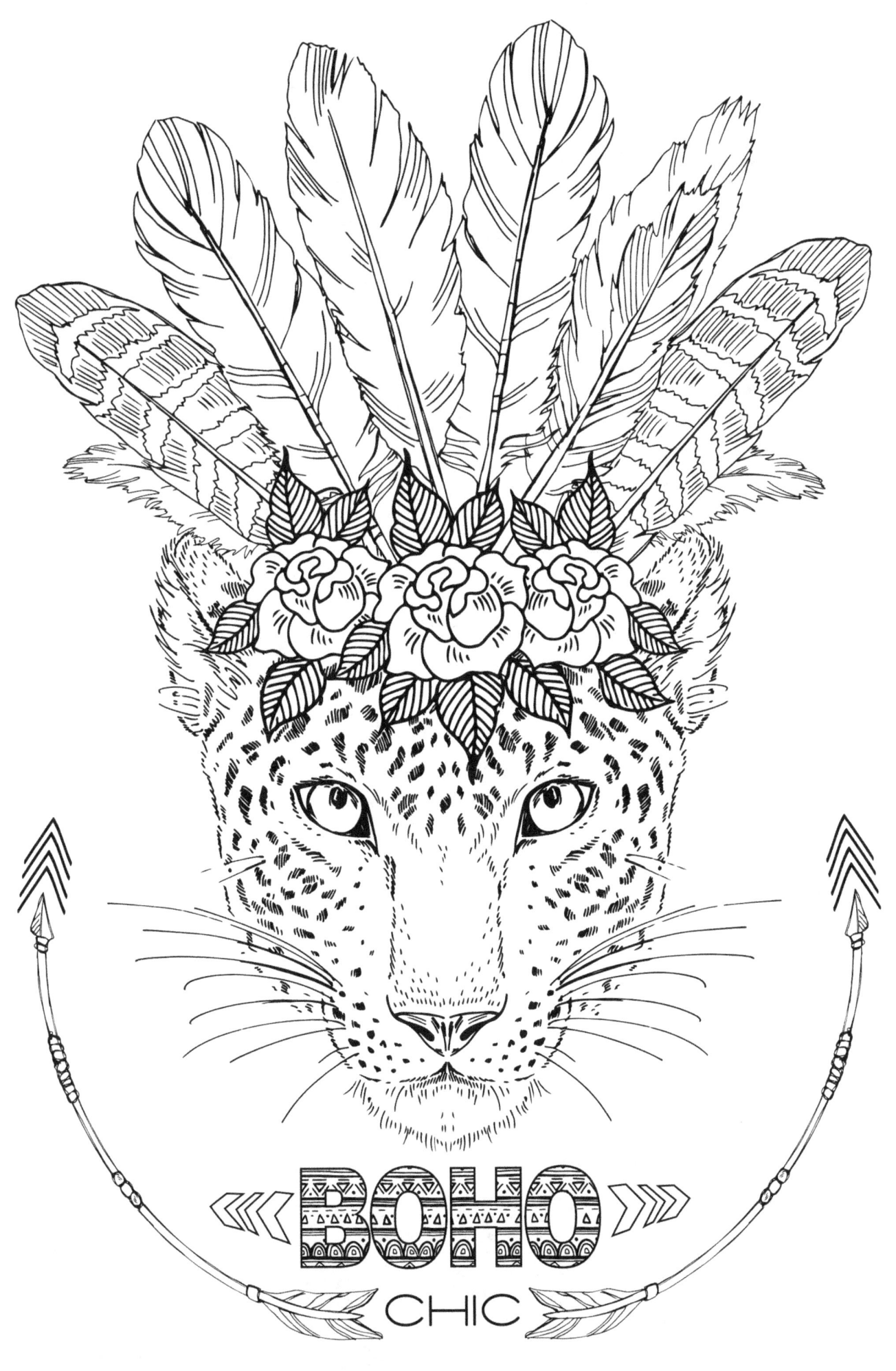

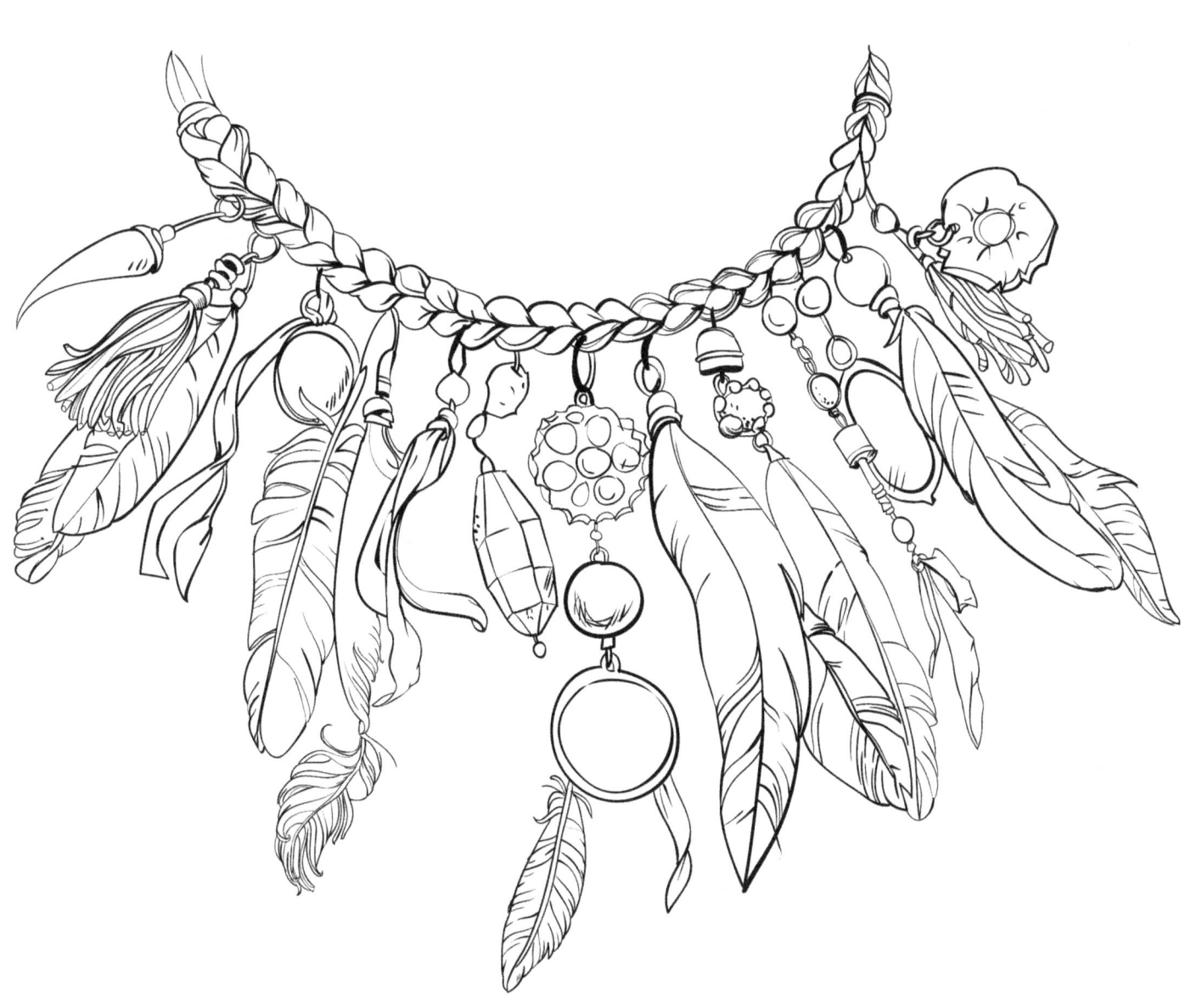

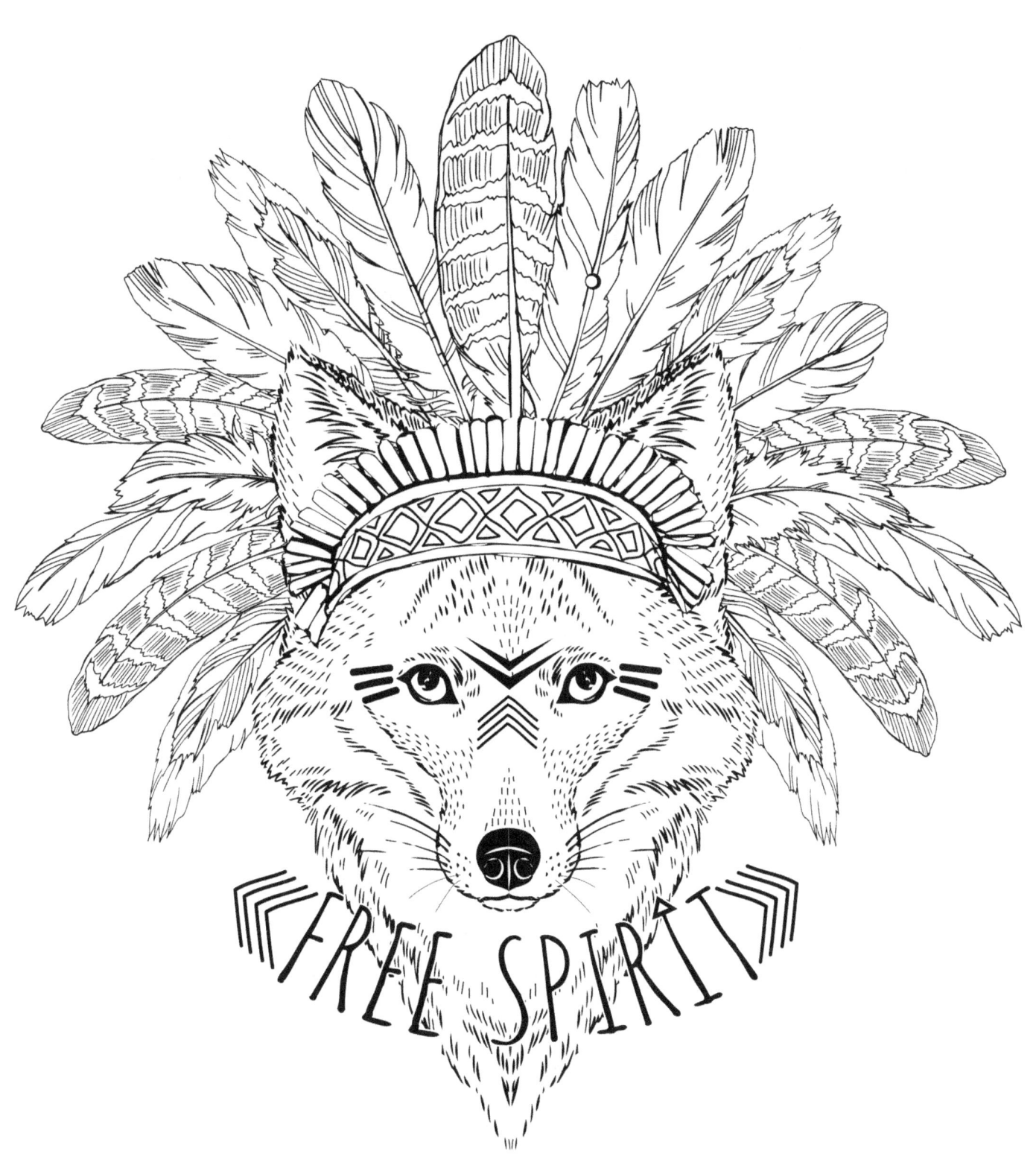

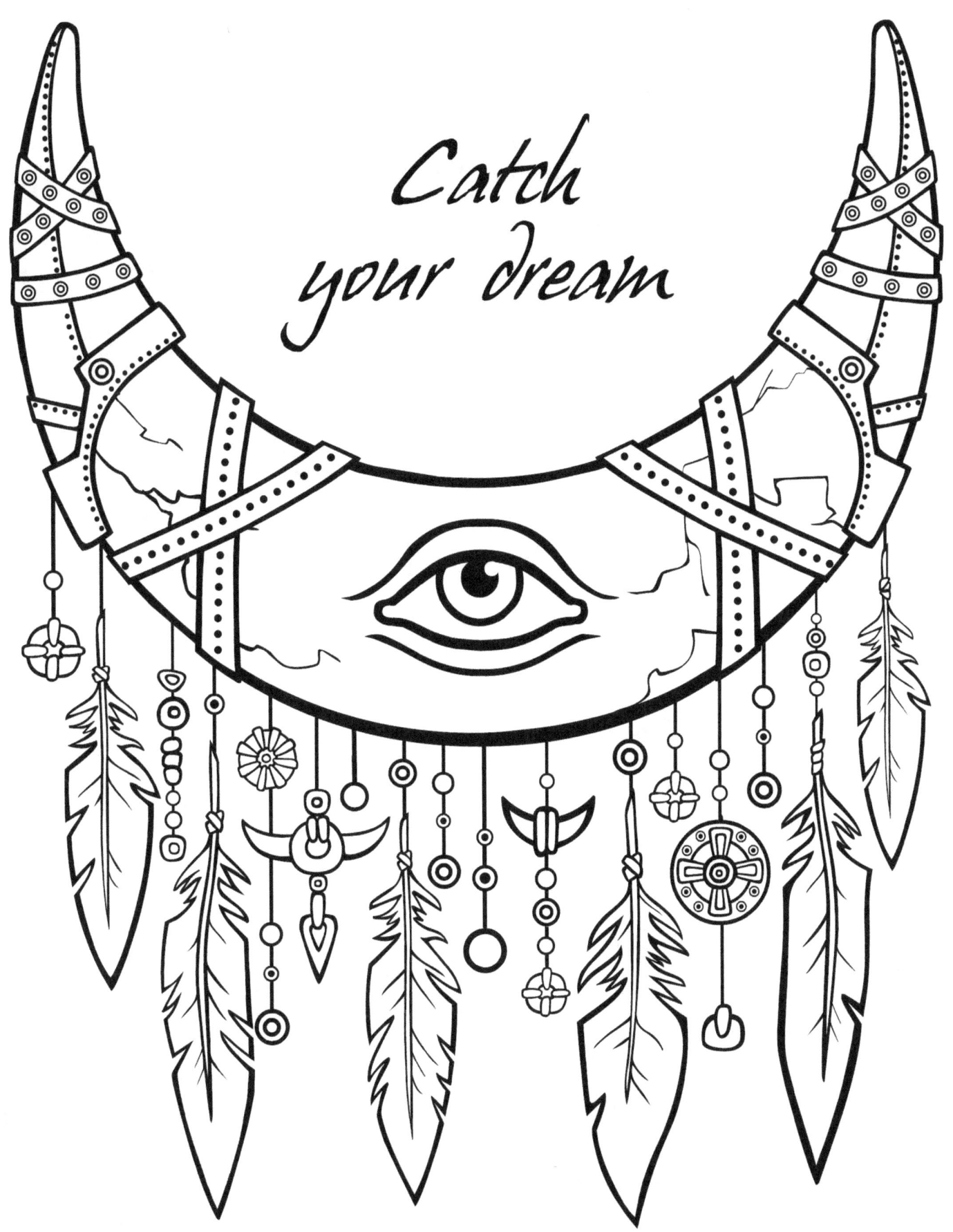

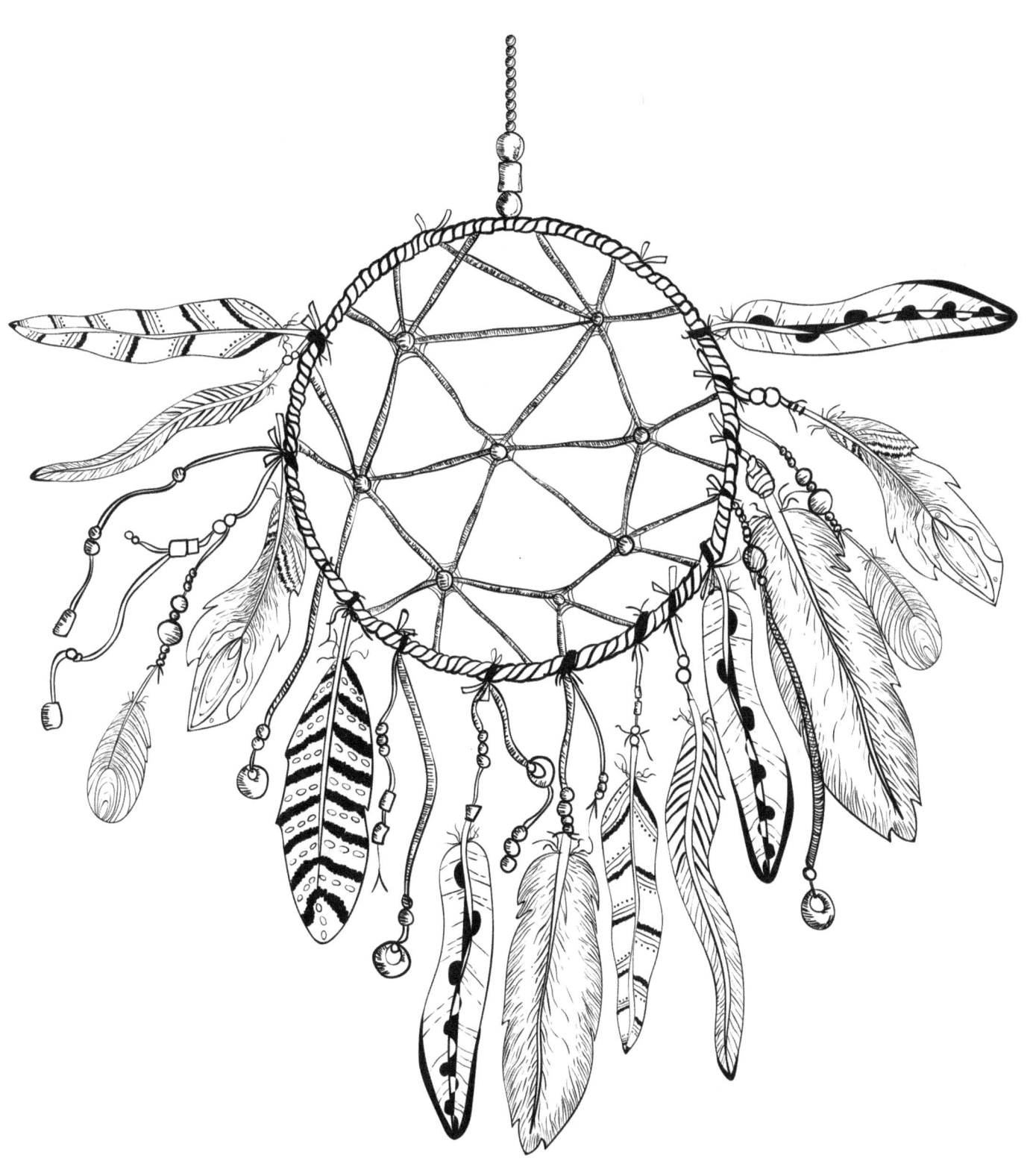

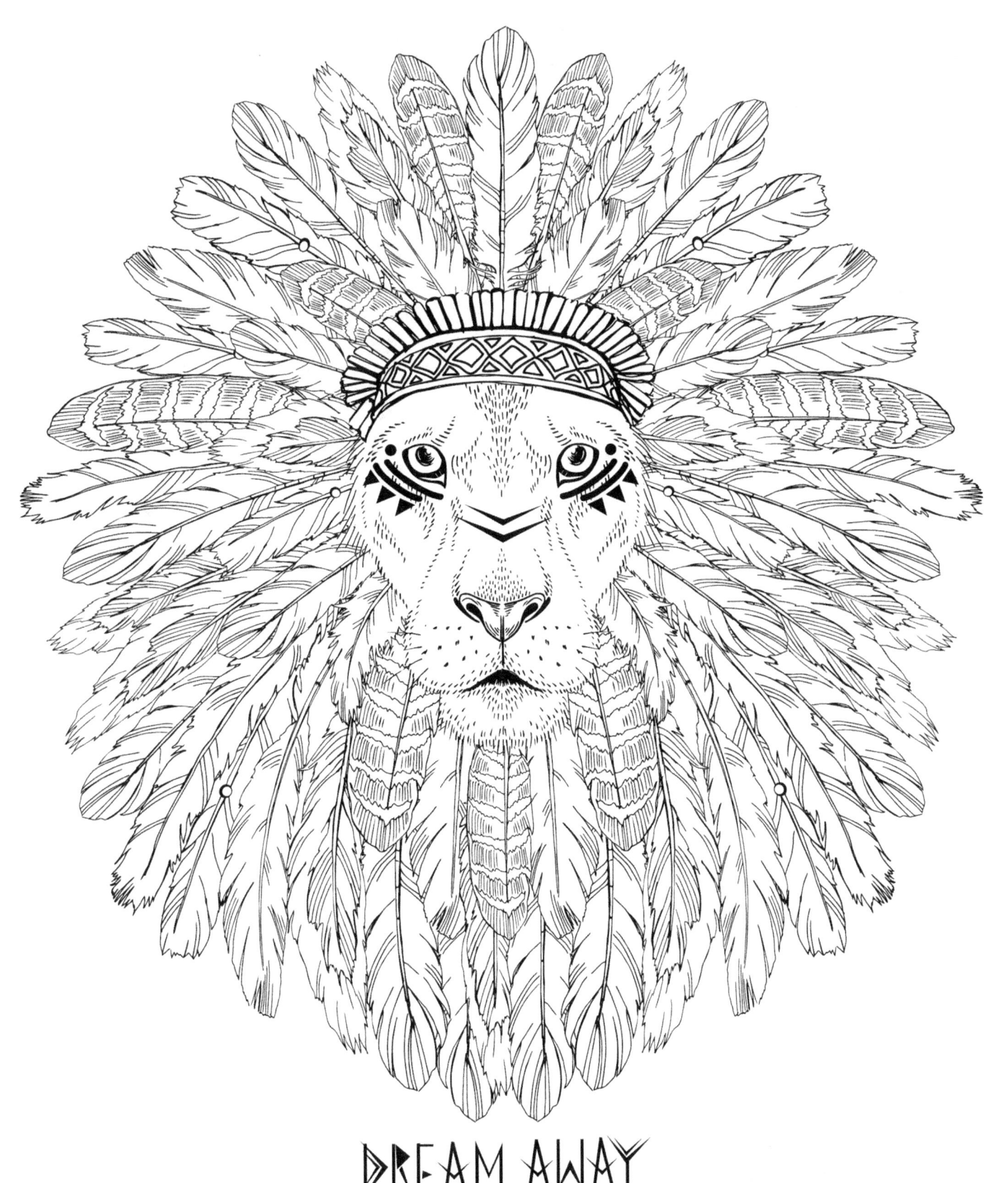

DREAM AWAY

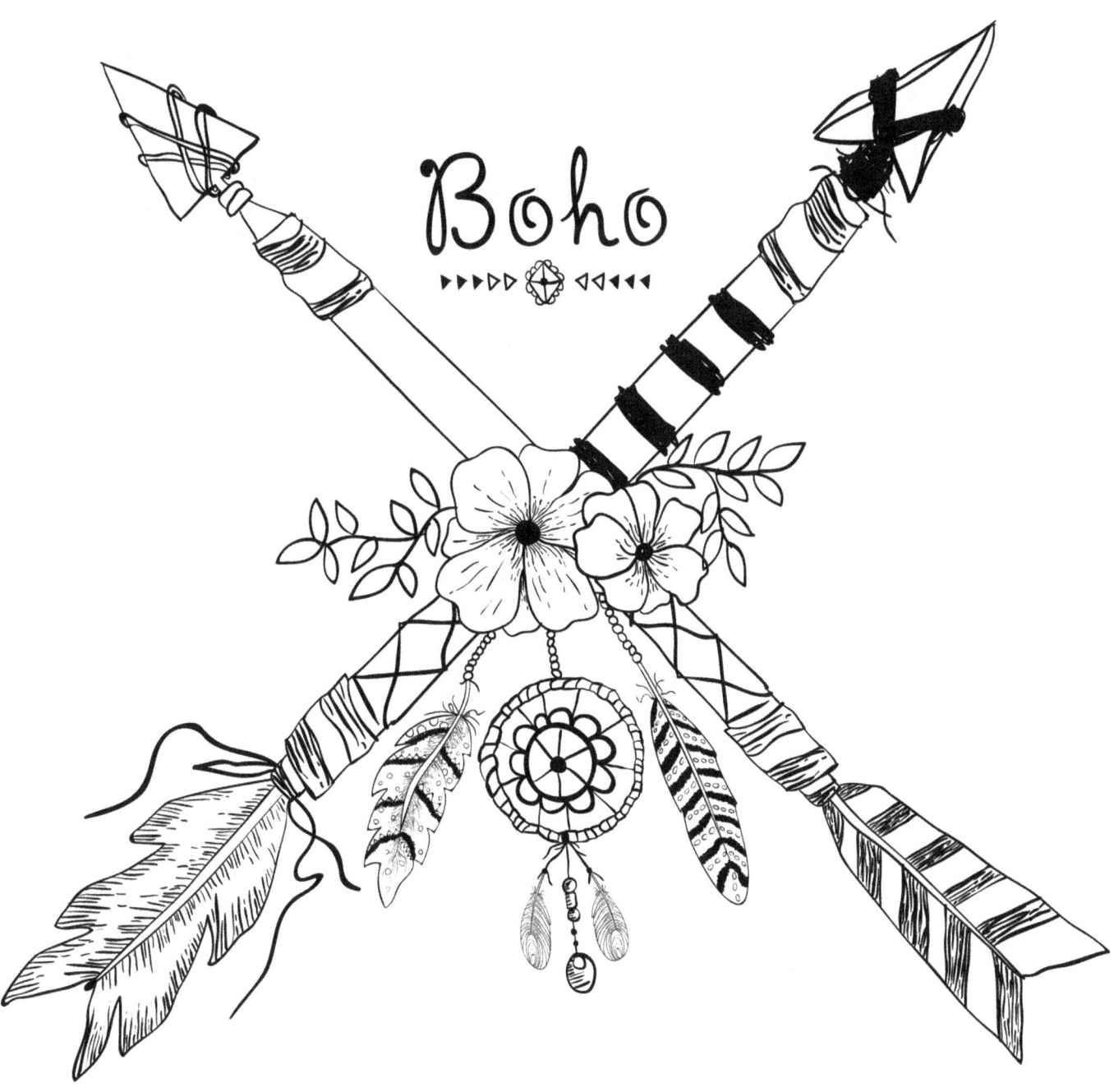

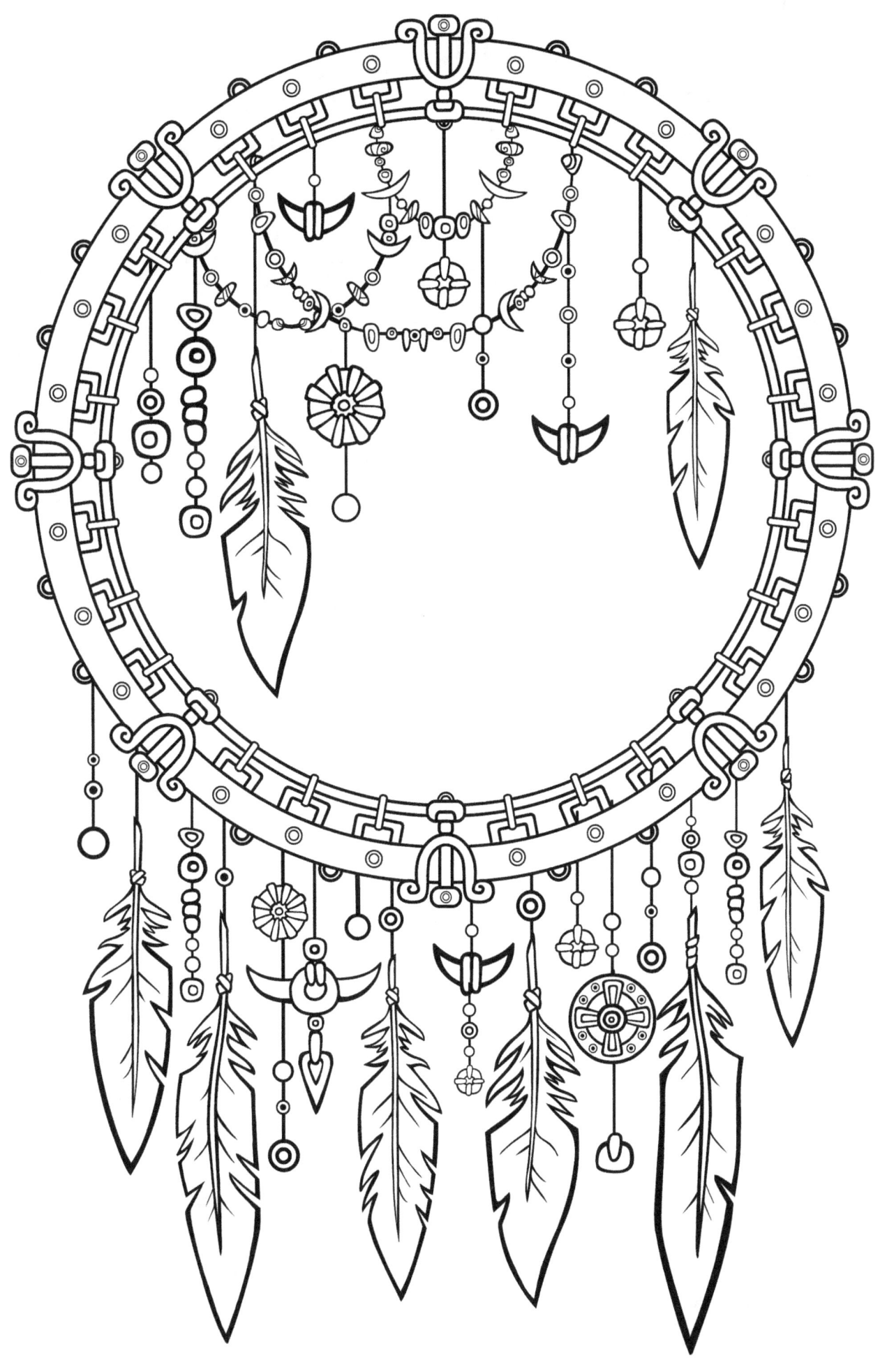

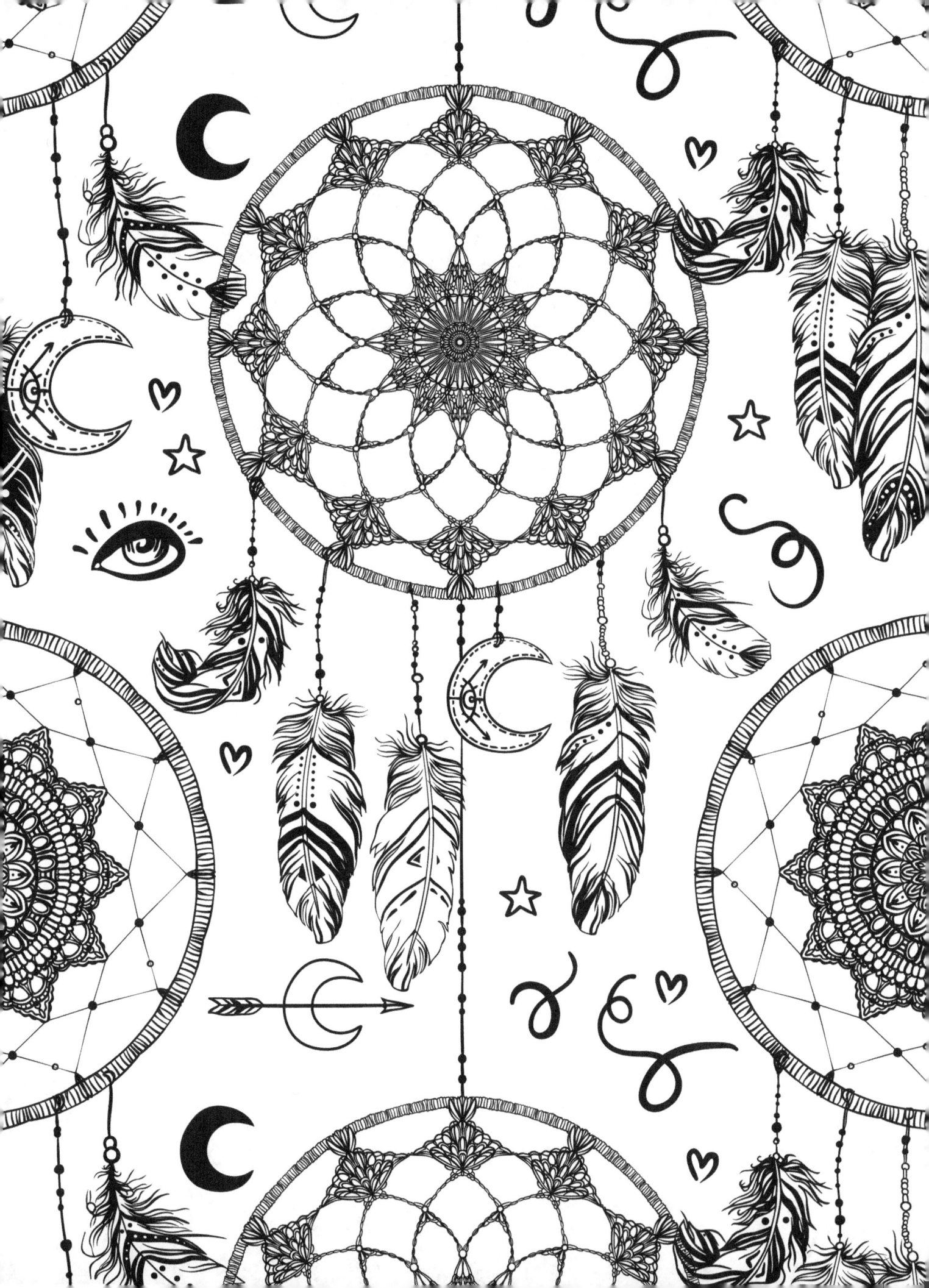

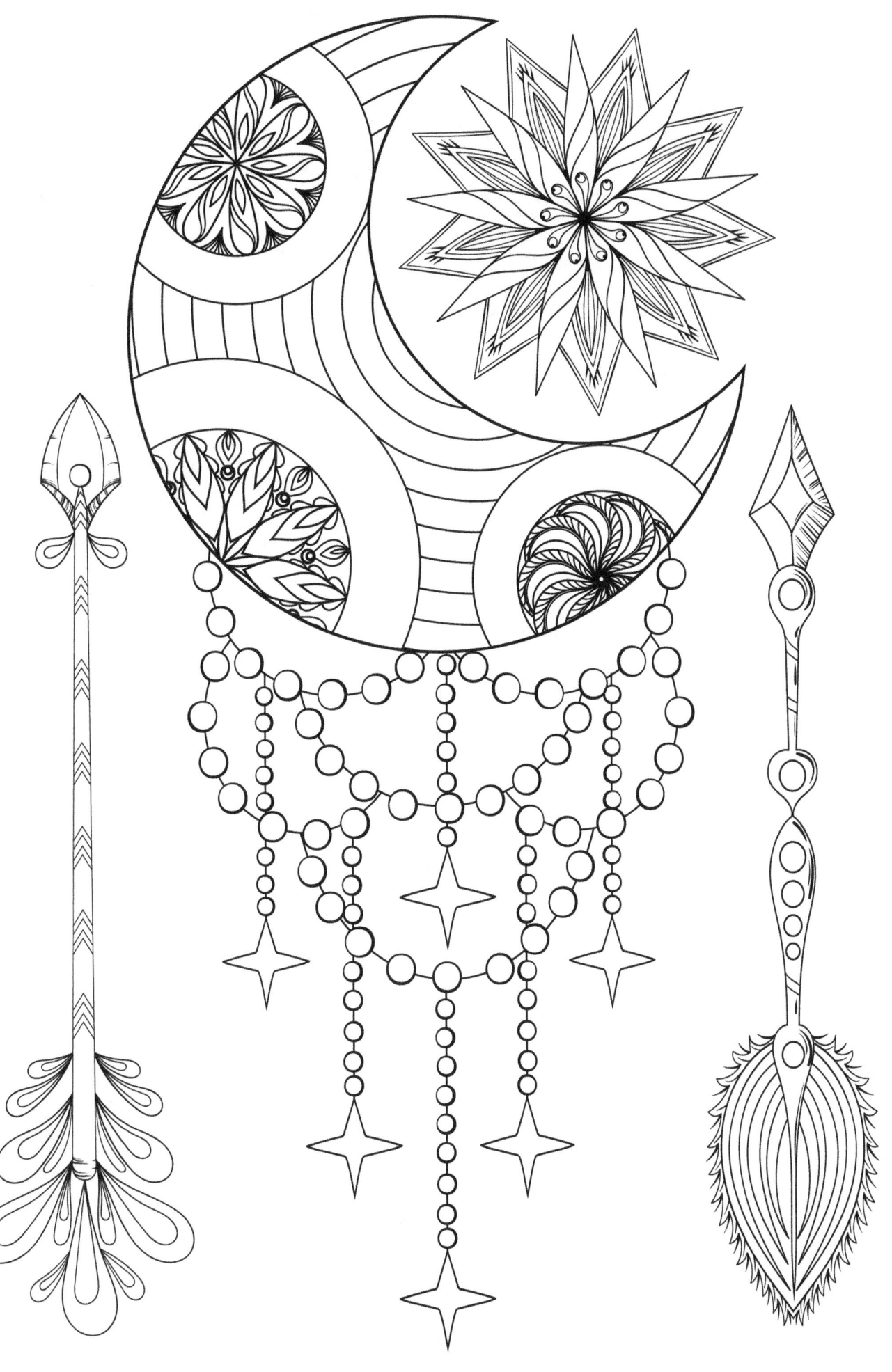

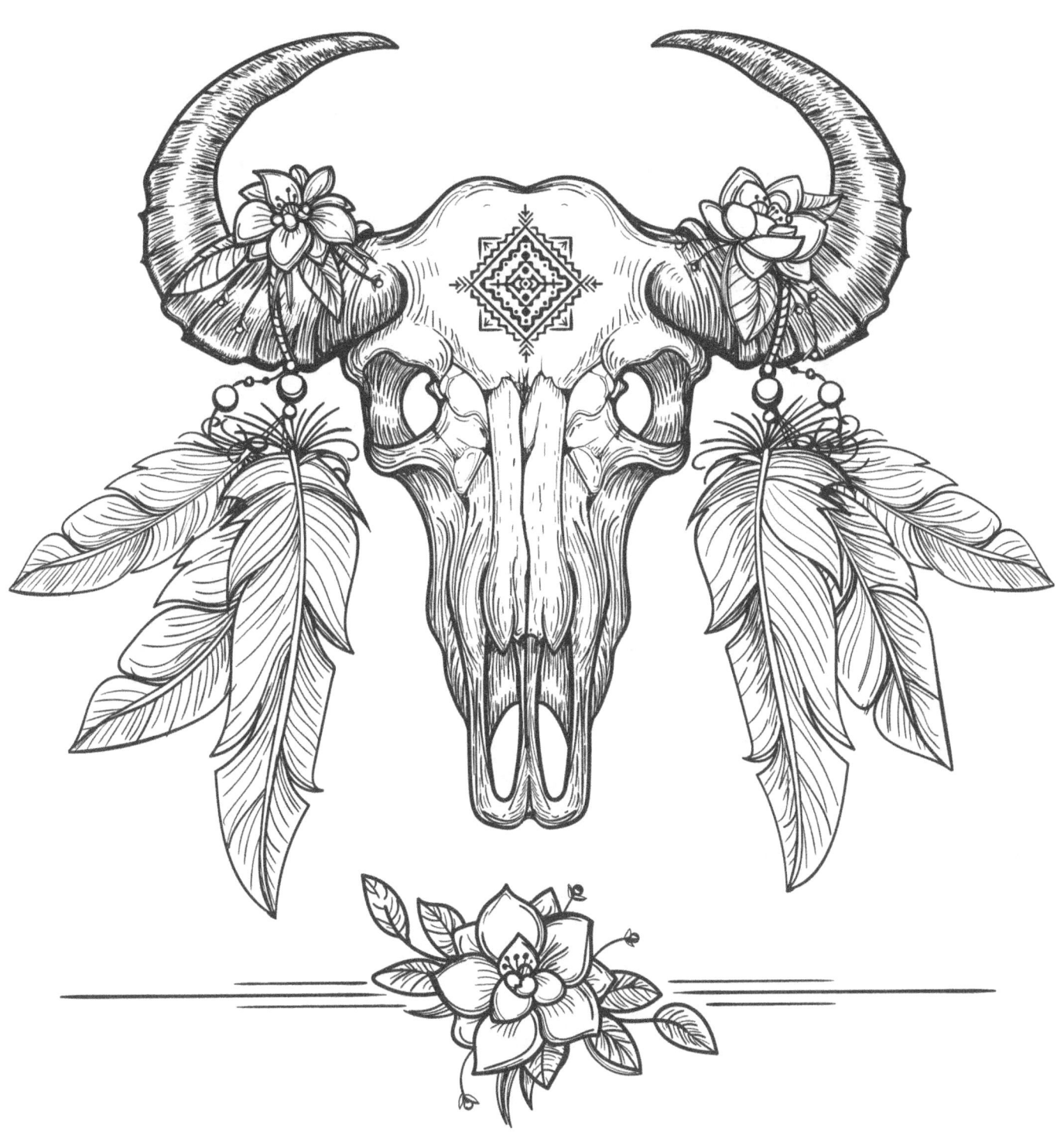

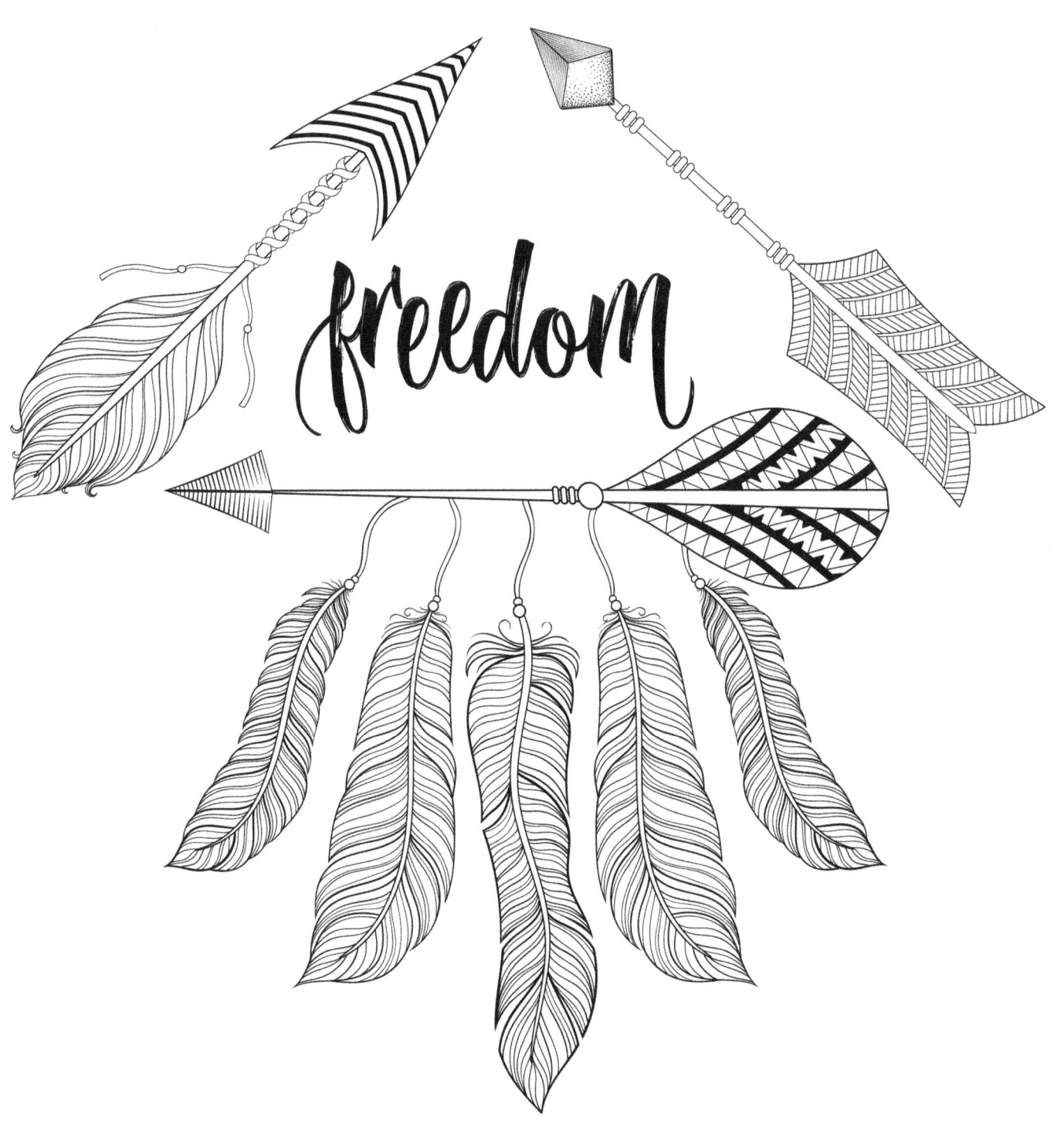

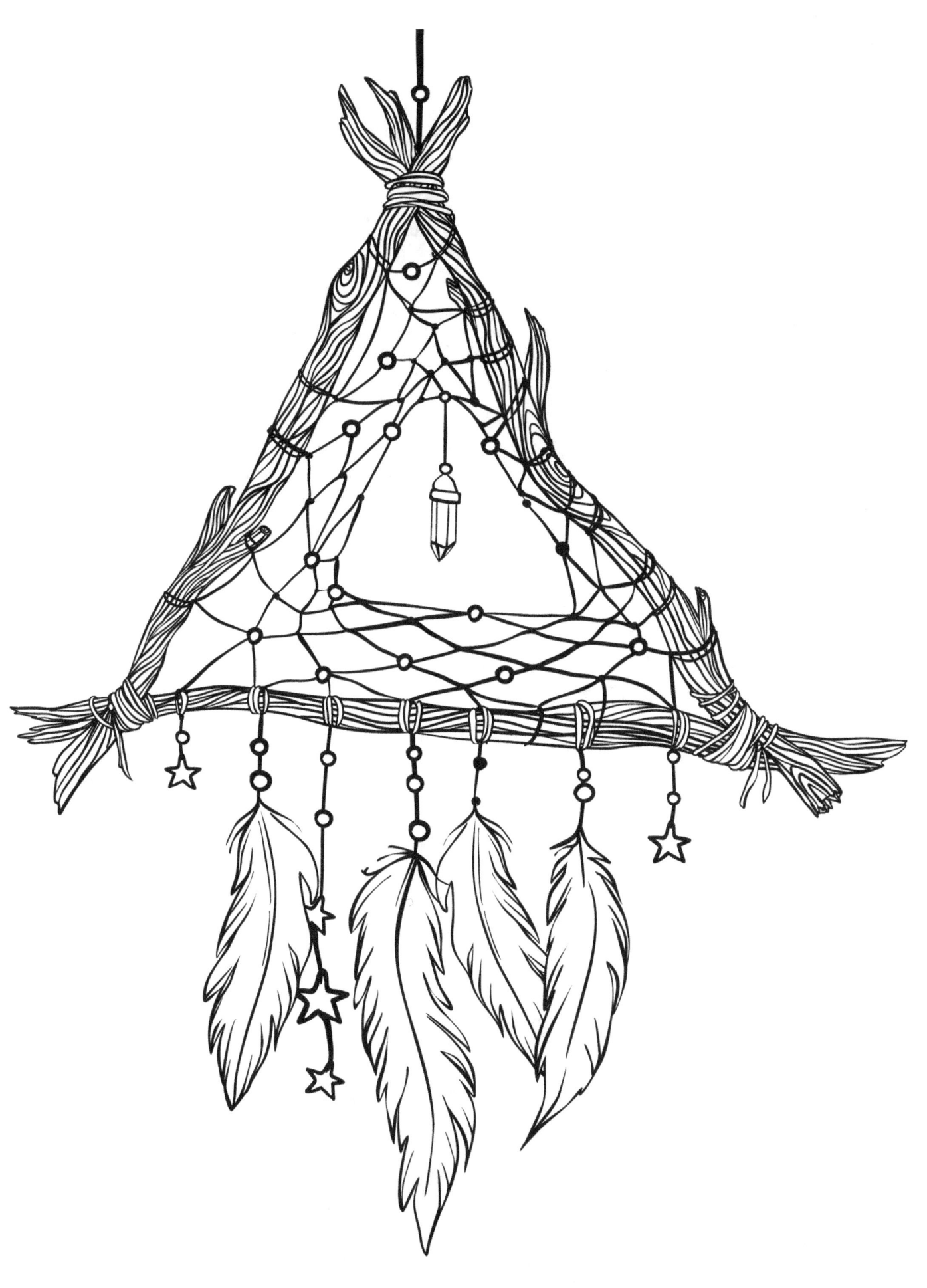

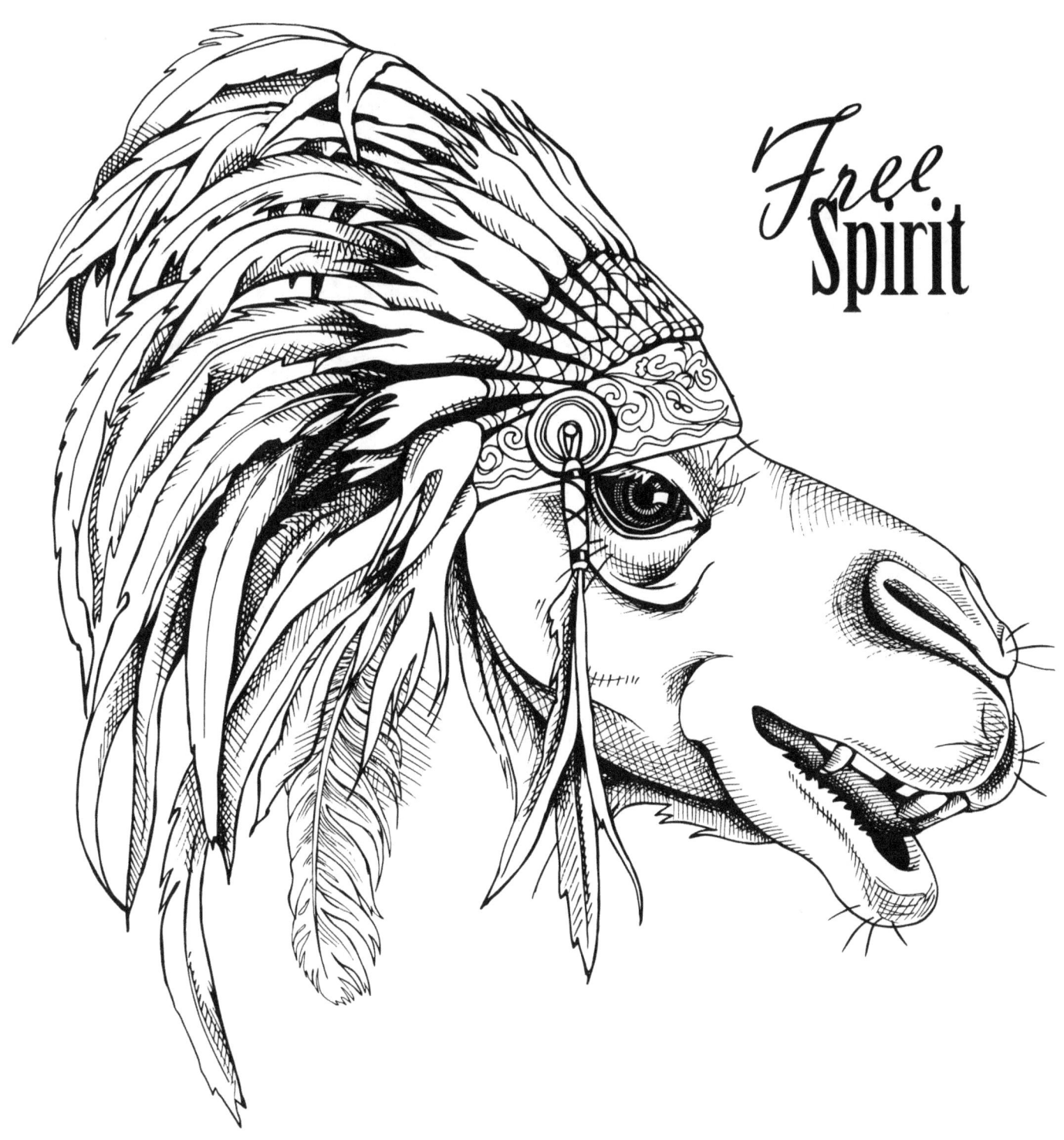

Free Spirit

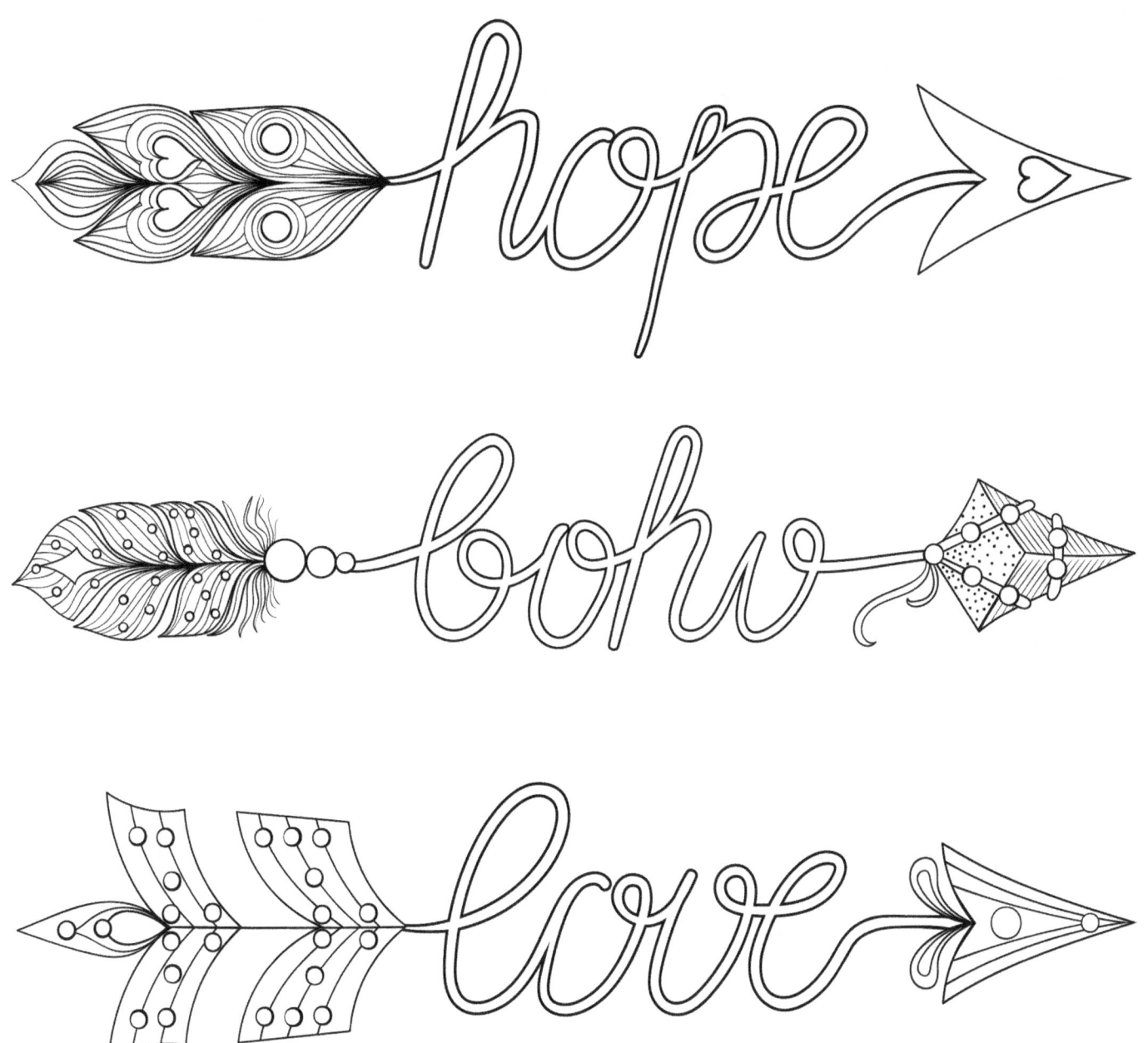

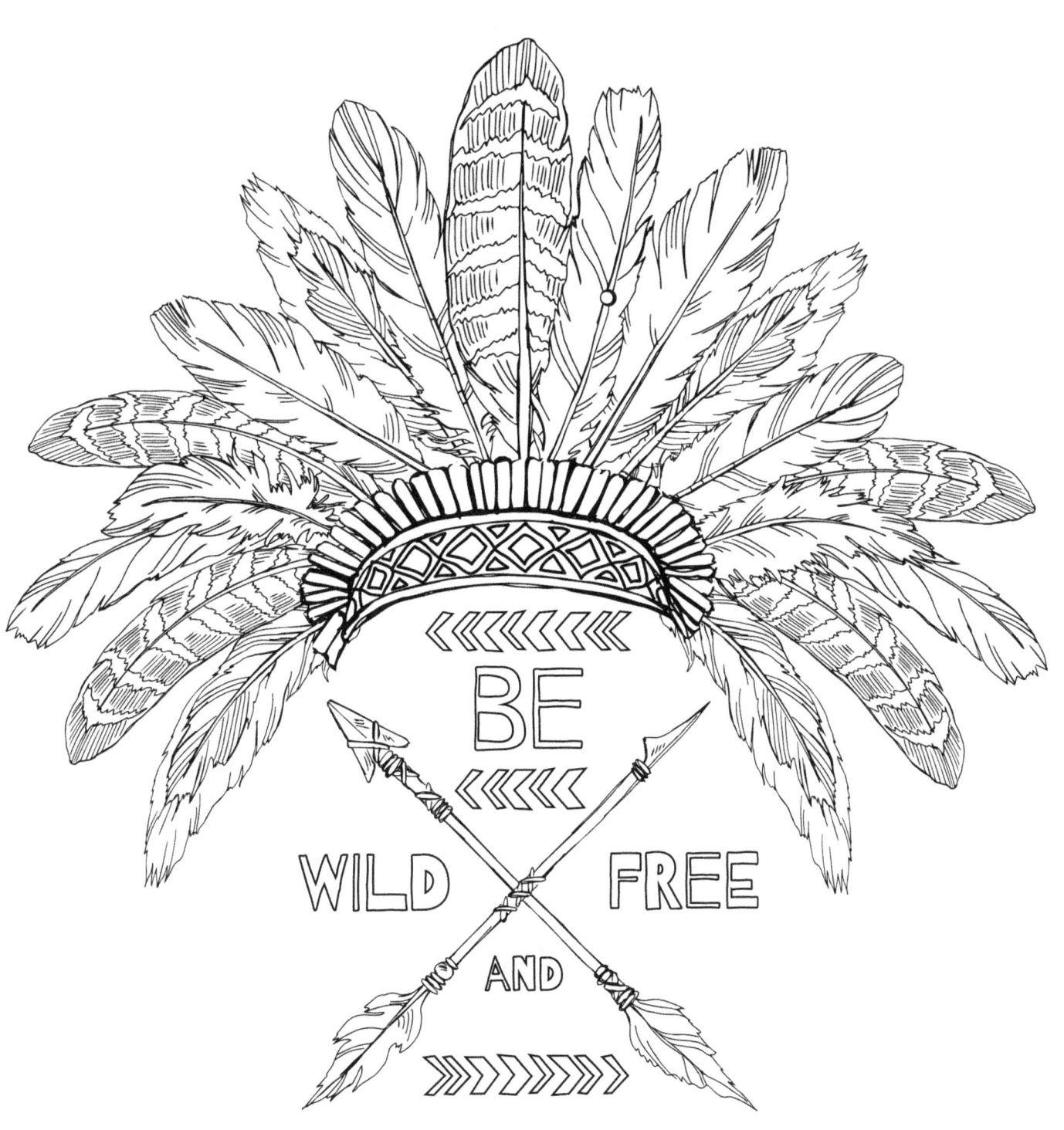

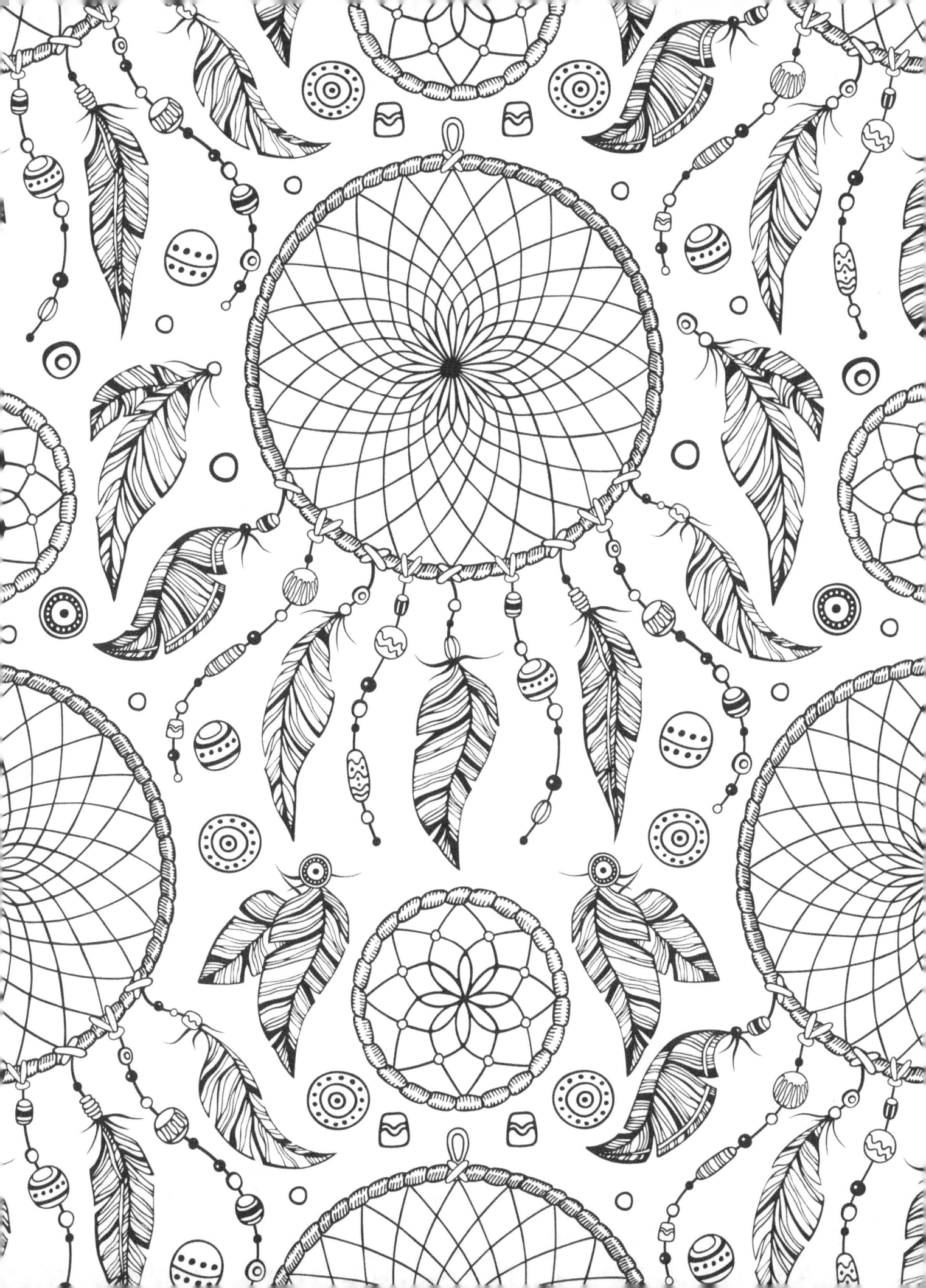

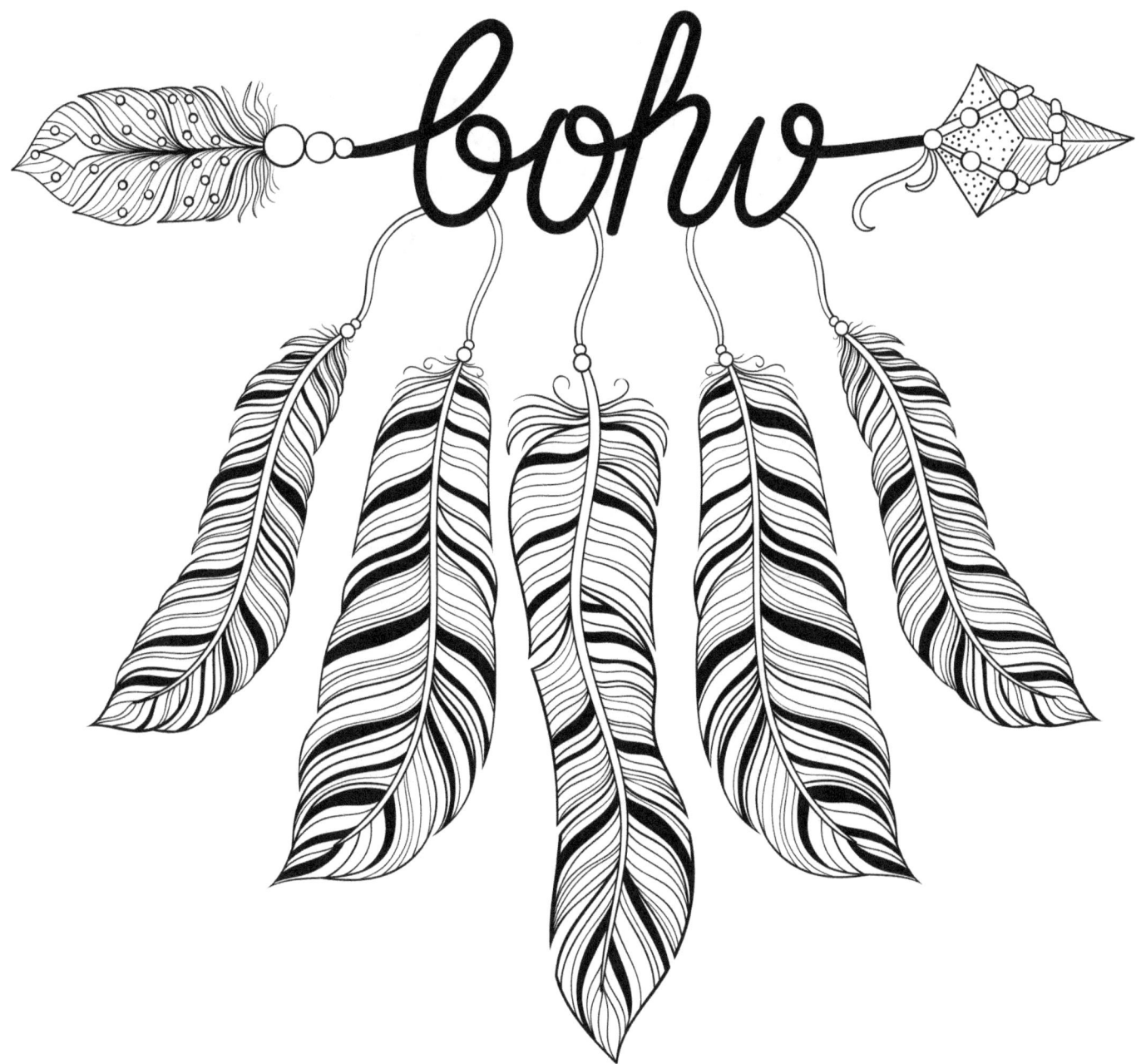

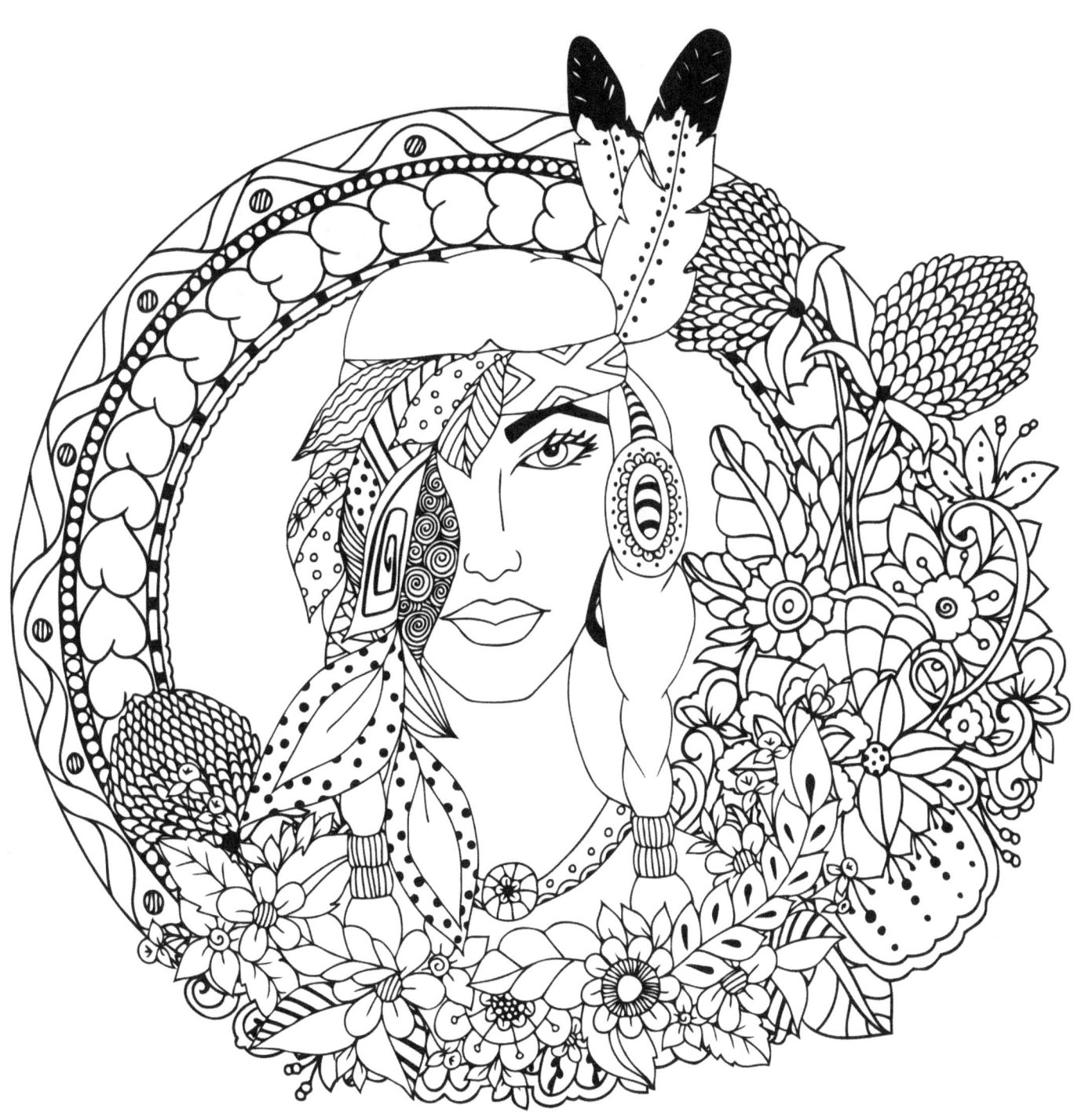

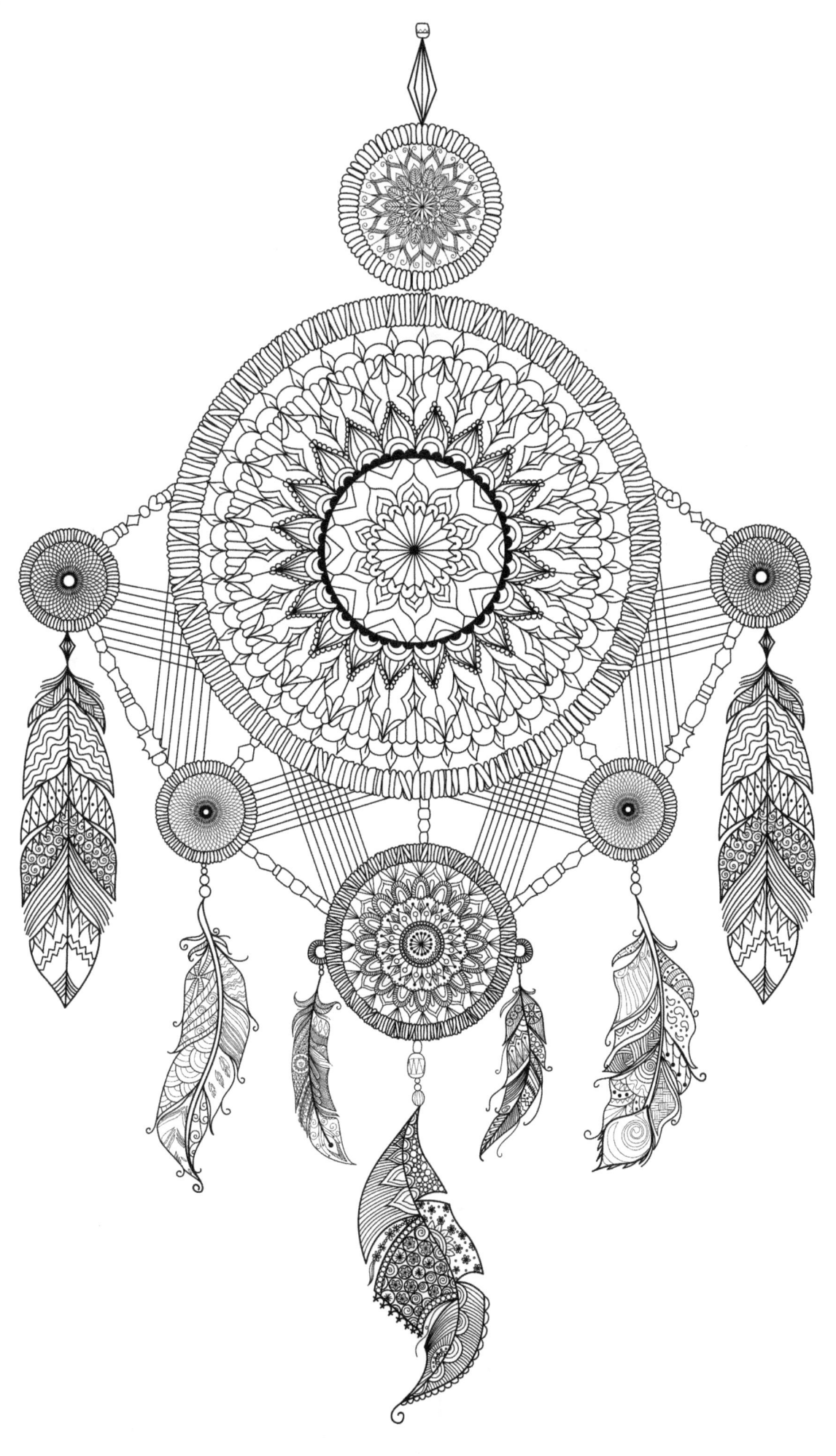

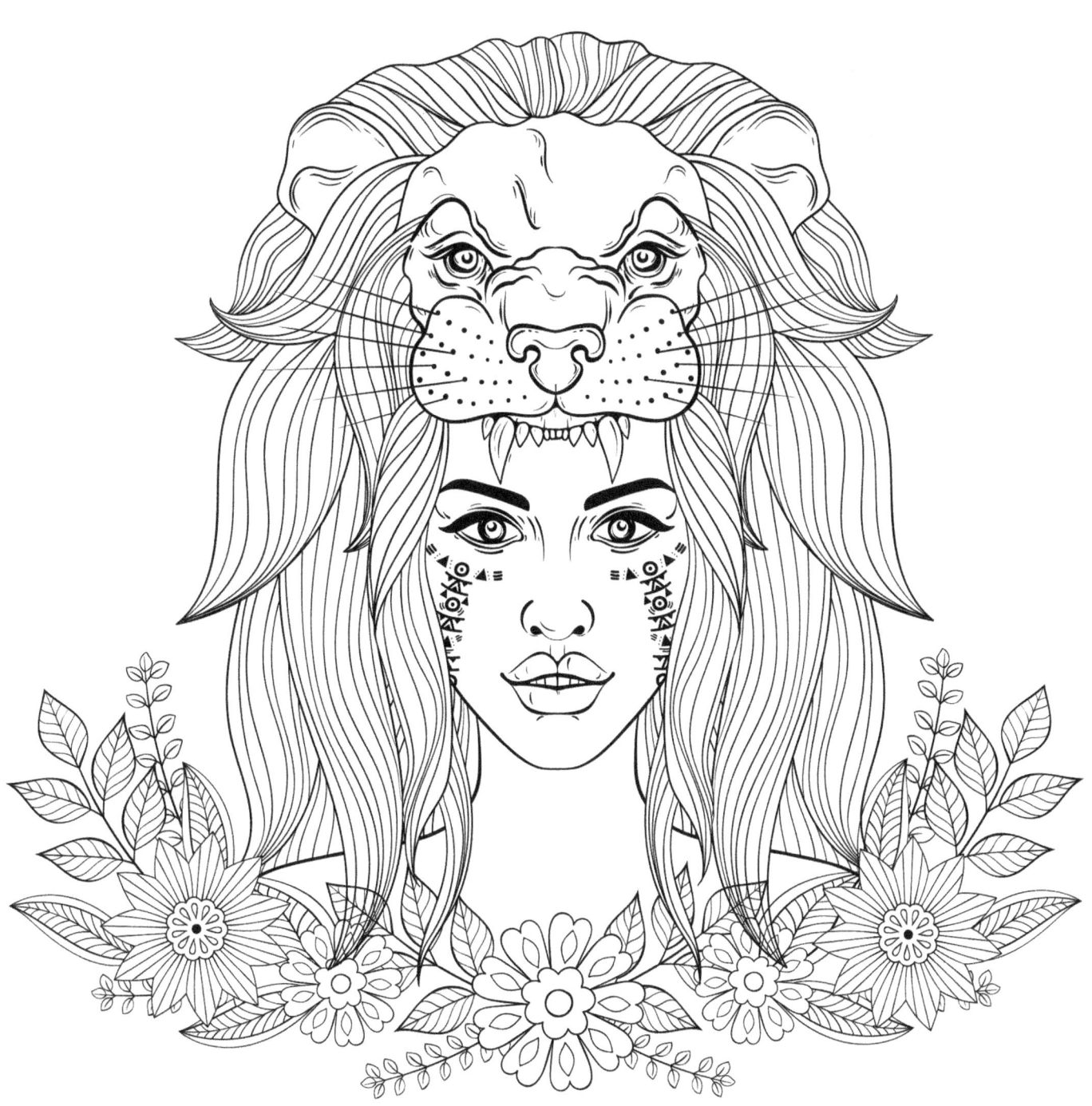

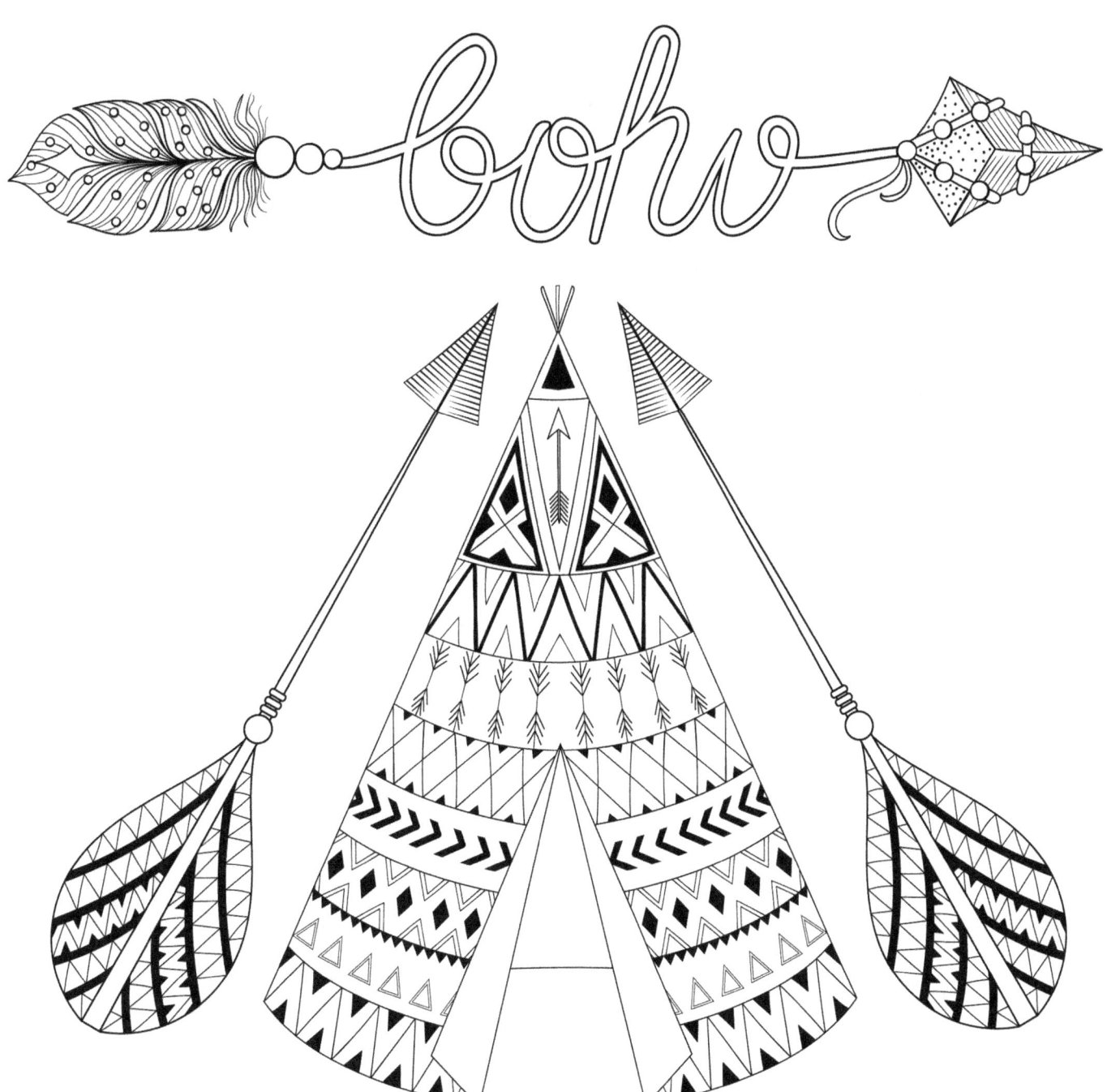

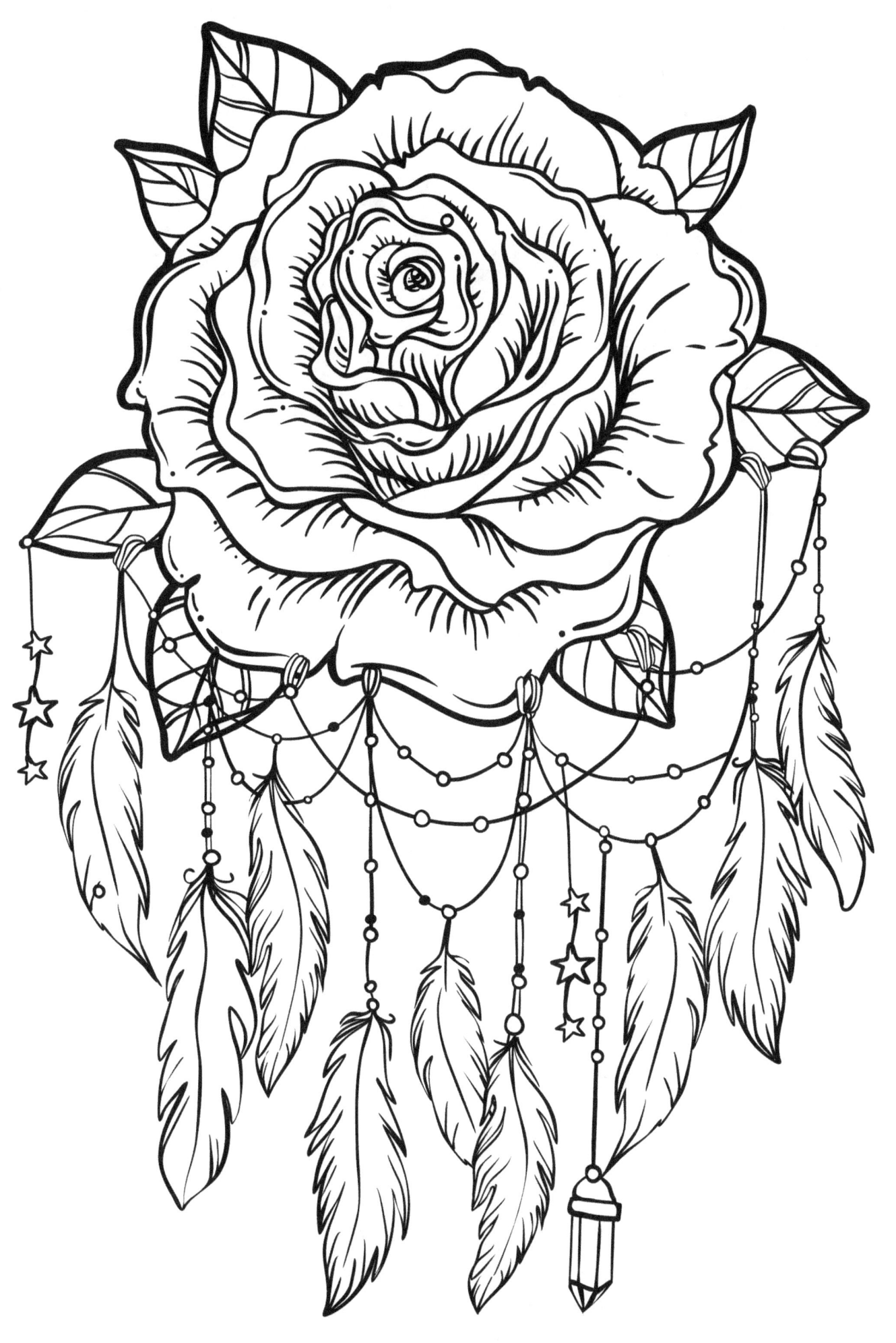

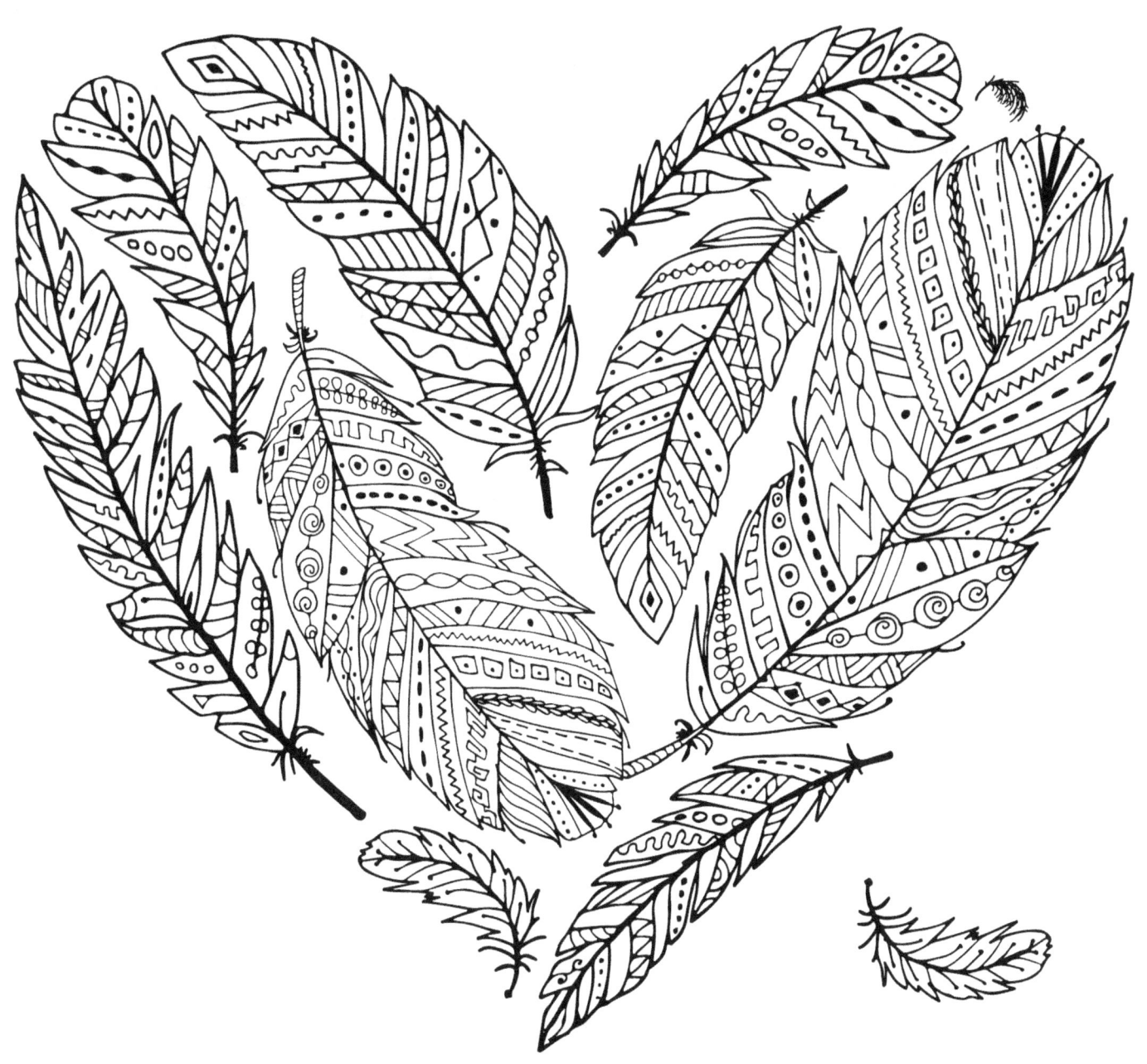

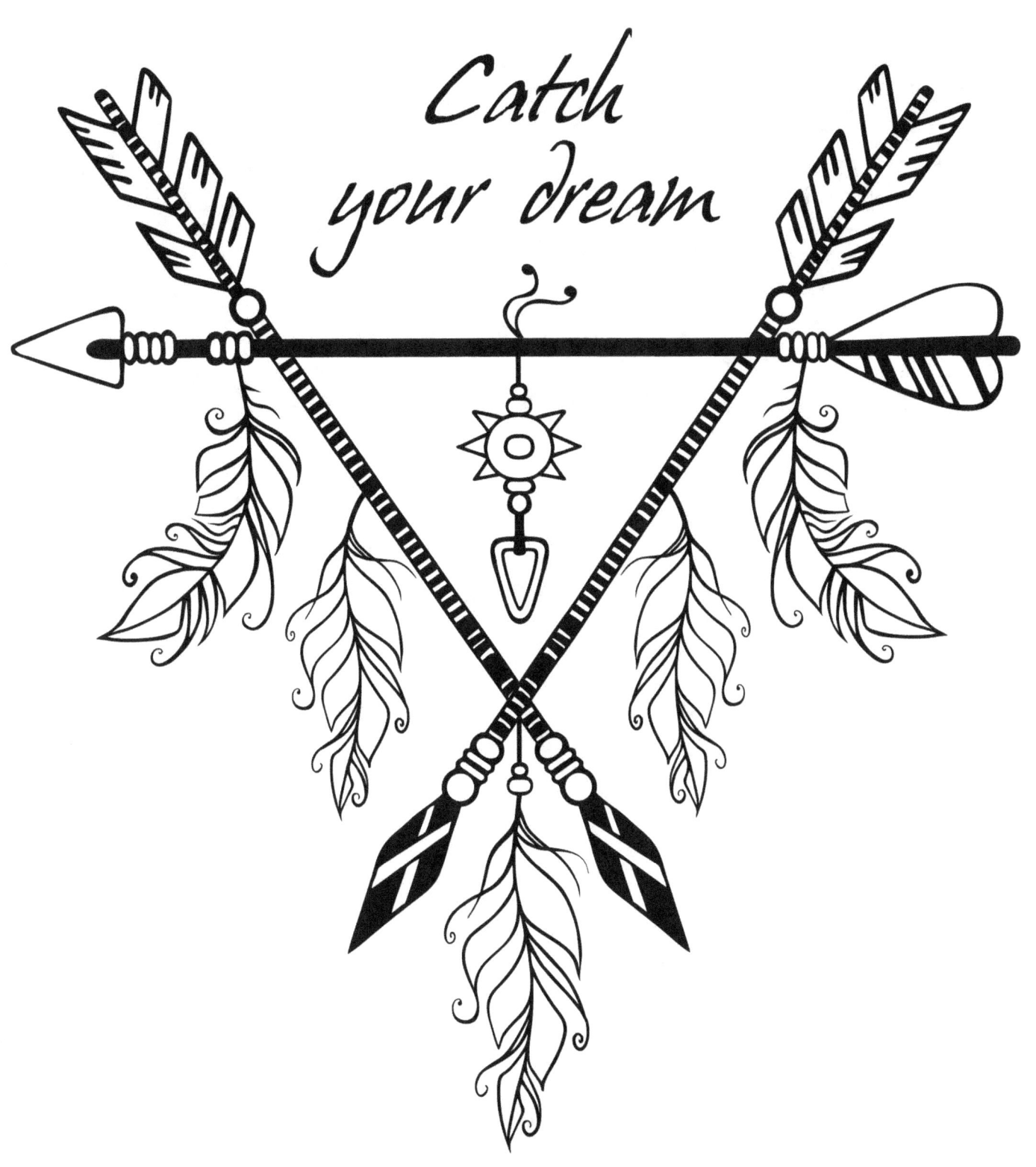

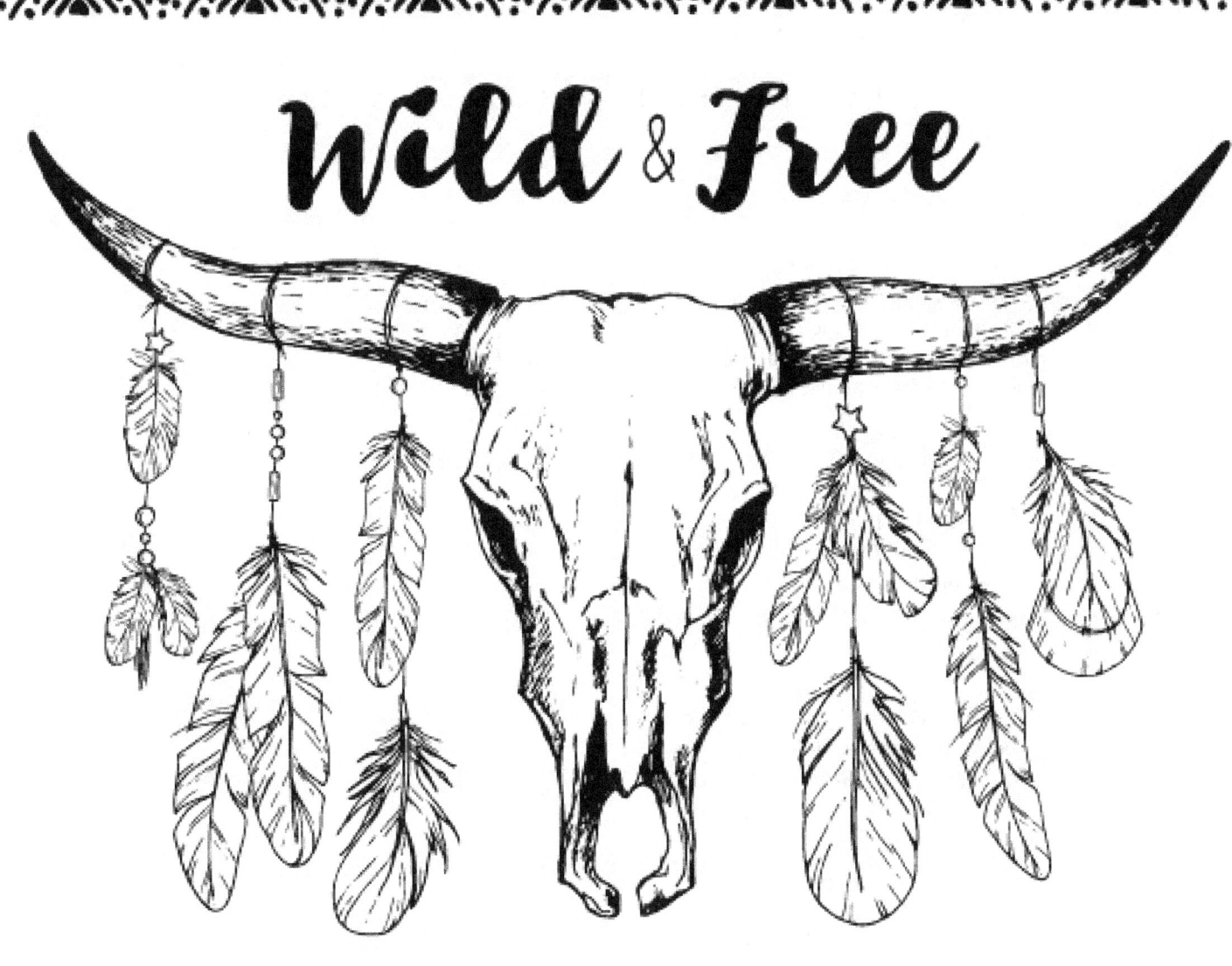

Best Selling Art Therapy Coloring Books

Coloring Books For Adults:

- Zombie Coloring Book: Black Background
- Butterfly Coloring Book For Adults: Black Background
- Tattoo Coloring Book: Black Background
- Coloring Books for Adults Relaxation: Native American Inspired Designs
- Fishing Coloring Book for Adults: Black Background

Coloring Books For Men:

- Coloring Book for Men: Anti-Stress Designs Vol 1
- Coloring Book For Men: Fishing Designs
- Coloring Book For Men: Tattoo Designs
- Coloring Books for Men: Hunting
- Coloring Book For Men: Biker Designs

Coloring Books For Seniors:

- Coloring Book For Seniors: Nature Designs Vol 1
- Coloring Book For Seniors: Anti-Stress Designs Vol 1
- Coloring Books for Seniors: Relaxing Designs
- Coloring Book For Seniors: Floral Designs Vol 1
- Coloring Book For Seniors: Ocean Designs Vol 1

Coloring Books For Teens and Tweens:

- Coloring Books For Teens: Ocean Designs
- Coloring Books for Teen Girls Vol 1
- Teen Inspirational Coloring Books
- Coloring Book for Teens: Anti-Stress Designs Vol 1
- Tween Coloring Books For Girls: Cute Animals

Coloring Books For Kids:

- Horse Coloring Book For Girls
- Coloring Books For Boys: Sharks
- Coloring Books for Boys: Animal Designs
- Unicorn Coloring Book for Girls
- Detailed Coloring Books For Kids

Art Therapy Coloring Books For Teens & Tweens

Coloring Books For Tweens

- Tween Coloring Book: Cute Animals Vols. 1–4
- Tween Coloring Book: Animal Designs Vols. 1–3
- Tween Coloring Book: Stress Relieving Designs
- Tween Coloring Book: Wolves, Lions, Tigers
- Tween Coloring Book: Dragon Designs
- Tween Coloring Book: Zendoodle Animals
- Tween Coloring Book: Black Background Vols. 1–3
- Tween Coloring Book: Heart Designs
- Tween Coloring Book: I Love You!!!
- Tween Coloring Book: Stress Relief Vols. 1–2
- Tween Coloring Book: Mermaid & Ocean Designs
- Tween Coloring Book: Ocean, Pirate, Skulls
- Tween Coloring Book: Ocean Designs Vols. 1–3
- Tween Coloring Book: Skull Designs
- Tween Coloring Book: Black Background Vols. 1–3
- Tween Coloring Book: Christmas Designs Vols. 1–4
- Coloring Book For Tweens: Fashion Girls
- Coloring Book For Tweens: Black Background Vols. 1–3
- Coloring Book For Tweens: Black Background Hearts
- Coloring Book For Tweens: Ocean Patterns Vols. 1–3

Coloring Books For Boys:

- Coloring Books For Boys: Animals
- Coloring Books For Boys: Dragons
- Coloring Books for Boys: Native American Inspired
- Coloring Books For Boys: Ocean Designs: Black Background
- Coloring Books For Boys: Wild Animals
- Coloring Books For Teen Boys: Detailed Designs: Black Background
- Coloring Books For Teen Boys: Detailed Designs
- Dinosaur Coloring Books For Boys: Detailed Designs
- Teen Boys Coloring Book: Animal Designs
- Teen Coloring Books For Boys: Detailed Designs: Black Background
- Teen Coloring Books For Boys: Detailed Designs

Art Therapy Coloring Books For Teens & Tweens

Coloring Books For Girls:

- Coloring Books For Girls: Cute Animals
- Coloring Books For Girls: Animals
- Coloring Books For Girls: Ocean Designs
- Coloring Books For Girls: Animal Designs
- Coloring Books For Girls: Unicorns
- Coloring Books For Girls: Princess & Unicorn Designs
- Coloring Book For Girls: Happy Birthday
- Coloring Books For Girls: 50 Cute Animals
- Coloring Books For Girls Relaxation: Black Background
- Coloring Books For Girls Relaxation: Butterflies
- Coloring Books For Girls Relaxation: Hearts
- Coloring Books For Teen Girls: Detailed Designs: Black Background
- Coloring Books For Teen Girls: Vols. 1–2
- Coloring Book For Teenage Girls: Fashion Faces
- Girls Coloring Books: Detailed Designs Vols. 1–2
- Girls Coloring Books: Cute Animals
- Adult Coloring Book For Girls: Detailed Designs
- Tween Coloring Book: Doodle Designs
- Teen Coloring Books For Girls Vols. 1–3

Coloring Books For Kids:

- Zombie Coloring Book For Kids
- Detailed Coloring Books For Kids: Butterflies: Black Background
- Detailed Coloring Books For Kids: Elephants
- Detailed Coloring Books For Kids: Geometric Designs
- Detailed Coloring Books For Kids: Ocean Designs
- Butterfly Coloring Book For Kids: Detailed Designs
- Detailed Coloring Books For Kids: Zoo Animals: Black Background
- Coloring Book For Kids Ages 8-12: Animals: Black Background
- Coloring Book For Kids: Cute Animals
- Coloring Book For Kids: Ocean Designs
- Heart Coloring Book For Kids
- Kids Mandala Coloring Book

Art Therapy Coloring Books For Teens & Tweens

Coloring Books for Teens:

- Coloring Books For Teens Relaxation: Dolphins & More
- Coloring Books For Teens Relaxation: Seahorses & More
- Coloring Books For Teens Relaxation: Sharks & More
- Coloring Books For Teens Relaxation: Wolves & More
- Coloring Books For Teens Relaxation: Nature Designs
- Coloring Book For Teens: Anti-Stress Designs Vols. 1–8
- Coloring Books For Teens: Cat & Dog Designs
- Coloring Books For Teens: Owls
- Teen Coloring Book: Inspirational Designs
- Teen Coloring Books: Music
- Teens Coloring Book: Ocean Theme
- Teen Coloring Books: Animal Designs
- Teen Coloring Books: Animals: Black Background
- Teen Coloring Books: Animal Designs: Black Background
- Adult Coloring Books For Teens: Animal Designs
- Detailed Coloring Book For Teenagers: Animal Designs
- Animal Coloring Book For Teens Vols. 1–2
- Butterfly Coloring Book For Teens
- Geometric Coloring Book For Teens
- Mandala Coloring Book For Teens: Black Background
- Mermaid Coloring Book For Teens: Black Background
- Motorcycle Coloring Book For Teens: Black Background
- Skull Coloring Book For Teens: Black Background
- Dinosaur Coloring Book For Teens: Black Background
- Christmas Coloring Book For Teens: Black Background

Coloring Books For Older Kids:

- Animal Coloring Book For Older Kids
- Coloring Books For Older Kids: Geometric Designs
- Coloring Books For Older Kids: Animal Designs
- Robot Coloring Book: Detailed Designs
- Wild Animals Coloring Book: Zendoodle Designs
- Zombie Coloring Book: Scary Designs: Black Background

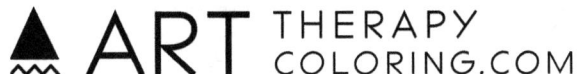

Drawing Page

Drawing Page

Drawing Page

Tween Coloring Books For Girls
Stress Relief Vol 1

Published by:
Art Therapy Coloring
www.arttherapycoloring.com